Sega Genesis Games
Secrets Greatest Tips
Second Edition

NOW AVAILABLE

Nintendo Games Secrets, Volumes 1, 2, 3, and 4
Nintendo Game Boy Secrets, Volumes 1 and 2
Nintendo Games Secrets Greatest Tips
Sega Genesis Game Secrets, Volumes 1, 2, 3, 4, and 5
Super NES Games Secrets, Volumes 1, 2, 3, and 4
Super NES Games Secrets Greatest Tips
Super Mario World Game Secrets
TurboGrafx–16 and TurboExpress Games Secrets, Volumes 1 and 2
The Legend of Zelda: A Link to the Past Game Secrets
Super Star Wars Official Games Secrets

COMPUTER GAME BOOKS

SimEarth: The Official Strategy Guide
JetFighter II: The Official Strategy Guide
The Official Lucasfilm Games Air Combat Strategies Book
Gunship 2000: The Official Strategy Guide
SimLife: The Official Strategy Guide
Stunt Island: The Official Strategy Guide
Lemmings: The Official Companion
Ultima: The Avatar Adventures
Ultima VII and Underworld: More Avatar Adventures
Populous: The Official Strategy Guide
A-Train: The Official Strategy Guide
X-Wing: The Official Strategy Guide
Prince of Persia: The Official Strategy Guide
F-15 Strike Eagle III: The Official Strategy Guide

How to Order:
Quantity discounts are available from the publisher, Prima Publishing, P.O. Box 1260BK, Rocklin, CA 95677; **(916) 632-4400** . On your letterhead include information concerning the intended use of the books and the number of books you wish to purchase.

Sega Genesis Games Secrets Greatest Tips
Second Edition

The Editors of
GamePro Magazine

Prima Publishing
P.O. Box 1260GBK
Rocklin, CA 95677

Library of Congress Catalog Number: 93-85024
ISBN: 1-55958-401-7

Executive Editor: Roger Stewart
Creative Director, Secret of the Games: Rusel DeMaria
Managing Editor: Neweleen A. Trebnik
Project Editor: Stefan Grünwedel
Cover Production Coordinator: Kim Bartusch
Design and layout: Marian Hartsough Associates
Editing and proofreading: LeeAnne McDermott
Cover design: Dunlavey Studio
Special Image Processing: Ocean Quigley

All products and characters mentioned in this book are trademarks of their respective companies.

94 95 96 97 RRD 10 9 8 7 6 5 4 3

Printed in the United States of America

Contents

ACKNOWLEDGMENTS

Thanks to Ryan, Kiley, and Matt for patience and understanding above and beyond the call of duty.
—L.M.

Introduction

Welcome to the second edition of *Sega Genesis Games Secrets Greatest Tips*. We've written this tip "encyclopedia" in response to the many calls and letters we get every day at *GamePro* Magazine. Most of the inquiries come from gamers wanting to know if we knew of a trick for a specific game. Answering all of those questions made us realize that, just like us, serious gamers would appreciate a book that enabled them to easily check to see if there were any tricks for whatever game they were currently playing.

In this book we've indexed and illustrated all of the secret tips, tricks, and passwords we know of for over one hundred different Sega Genesis games. Inside these pages you'll find our collected game secrets in alphabetical order, including updated tricks for the most popular games. All you have to do is look up the title of the game you're interested in and you'll find whatever tricks of the trade we know for that particular title!

And there's more. We've also included a section of tricks which we at *GamePro* refer to as "Yank the Cart Tricks." These tricks can make some amazing things happen to your game, but please read our words of warning. Performing these tricks can damage your Sega Genesis system—so, as always, perform them at your own risk.

Finally, we've included an updated section with codes for two of the handiest hardware helpers to come down the video pipeline in quite some time. The Action Replay and Pro Action Replay can enhance your game play in some ways you might never have imagined possible. Enjoy!

Psst . . . remember, you're the pros! If you've got any tricks of the trade that we missed, send them to:

Secret Weapons
GamePro Magazine
P.O. Box 5828
San Mateo, CA 94402

If we use your trick, you'll find your name on the pages of *GamePro* Magazine and we'll send you a *GamePro* super shirt!

Part I

Sega Genesis Games
Secrets Greatest Tips—
from *A* to *Z*

✦ After Burner II ✦

Level Select

Soar to any level in *After Burner II* with this Level Select trick. Wait until the Title screen with the words "Start/Options" appears on-screen. Then, simultaneously press and hold Buttons A, B, and C on your control pad and then press Start two times. When the words "Select Stage" appear on-screen, use Left and Right on your control pad to choose any stage up to 20.

Bonus Missiles

Power up with this extra missile code for *After Burner II*. Hold down the following buttons for each round during the refueling sequence. You'll up your missiles to 100!

Round 3: Left and Button B
Round 5: Right and Button B
Round 9: Button B
Round 11: Right and Button B
Round 13: Left and Button B
Round 16: Right and Button B
Round 19: Button B
Round 21: Right and Button B

✈ Air Diver ✈

Invincibility

You won't need to dive for cover with this Invincibility trick for *Air Diver*. Begin your game and head for an area where there are no enemies on-screen. Next, press and hold Start while you press Button A, Button B, Button C, Button B, Button A two times, Button B, Button C,

Button B, Button A, and Button B. Finally, release Start and then press it again and hold it until the next round starts. Now you're invincible!

♟ Alex Kidd in the Enchanted Castle ♟

Continue

You can continue in *Alex Kidd in the Enchanted Castle*—but not until you have 1,000 or more Baums of gold!!

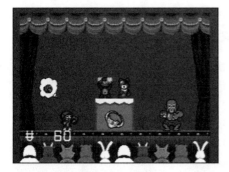

Win at Janken

Winning at Janken is important if you're going to outwit Ashra in the Enchanted Castle. Here's what to do: Keep switching your hand as fast as you can until the game stops. Remember that you've got a

66% chance of either winning or tying, so the odds are in your favor. And remember, once you have the Necklace, use it to read your opponent's mind and win with ease.

Rookietown Level Underground Passage

There are many secret passages in *Alex Kidd in the Enchanted Castle*. To discover the secret passage in Rookietown, jump on the ground

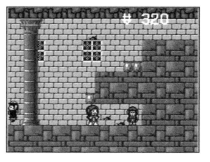

near the second palm tree just past the first Janken House. You'll find Bonus Items, including a 1-Up, down below.

Prairie Level Underground Passage

You'll find the Prairie's secret passage underneath an orange treasure chest. The treasure chest you're looking for is the next chest past the one guarded by the Eagle, inside of a pyramid-shaped set of blocks. Break the treasure chest to enter. You'll find more Bonus Items inside this treasure room, including a 1-Up.

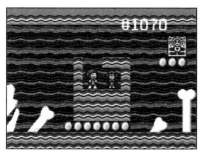

Tropicstown Level Underground Passage

Look for the secret passage in Tropicstown underneath the first black treasure chest you reach. Just smash the treasure chest and enter the passage to search for Power-Ups and a 1-Up.

Castle Shortcut

The Enchanted Castle is a Kidd killer, but there's a shortcut that Alex can use to make things easier. When you reach the Castle area, fly the Pedicopter up and to the right to a secret ledge on the outside of the Castle. When you reach the

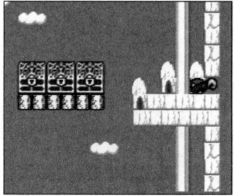

ledge, lie on your stomach and punch the wall to make an opening. Crawl inside and you'll begin part-way through the Castle.

Another Castle Shortcut

There's another shortcut near the end of the Castle. Go to the area where you can purchase the Cape. Climb on top of the door and use your Pogo stick to leap into the air and snag a few coins. Now, crawl to the right and punch the wall of the

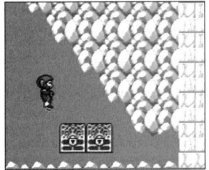

Castle. Enter the Castle and quickly flip the switch to stop the descending ceiling. Move to the right and punch the walls. In the next room flip the first switch, and then enter Ashra's chambers for the final battle.

☆ Alien Storm ☆

Life After Death

This cool *Alien Storm* trick may make you believe in reincarnation. Once you've earned enough energy to do your special

move and you're playing as the robot Scooter, you're ready to roll. Use your special attack move as you die. You won't have any energy left, but you won't be dead! As long as you continue to power up your Life again you can do this trick every time you die.

✂ Alisia Dragoon ✂

Tons of Pad Tricks

Alisia's one of the unsung, lesser-known heroines of the Genesis. There are a ton of codes hidden in this great little game. To access them, wait until the Sega logo disappears from the screen, and then press and hold Button A. Continue to hold A until the words

"Produced by Game Arts" disappear from the screen. Let go of A and then press and hold Button B. Continue to hold B until the words "Associated with Gaimax" disappear from the screen. Then, press and hold Button C until the words "Music Composed by Menaco Associates" disappears from the screen. Finally, press and hold Start. If you've performed the trick correctly, you'll hear a musical tone. When your regular game begins, the following pad tricks can be executed at any time!

Warps

> **Stage Skip:** Press Button C on Controller 2.
>
> **Warp to Stage 1:** Press Button C on Controller 2, then press and hold Button C on Controller 2.
>
> **Warp to Stage 2:** Press Button C on Controller 2, then press and hold Button B on Controller 2.
>
> **Warp to Stage 3:** Press Button C on Controller 2, then press and hold Buttons B and C on Controller 2.

Warp to Stage 4: Press Button C on Controller 2, then press and hold Button A on Controller 2.

Warp to Stage 5: Press Button C on Controller 2, then press and hold Buttons A and C on Controller 2.

Warp to Stage 6: Press Button C on Controller 2, then press and hold Buttons A and B on Controller 2.

Warp to Stage 7: Press Button C on Controller 2, then press and hold Buttons A, B, and C on Controller 2.

Warp to Stage 8: Press Button C on Controller 2, then press and hold Start on Controller 2.

Power-Ups

Refill Damage Meter: Press Button A on Controller 2, then press and hold Up on Controller 1 and press Button B on Controller 2.

Increase Thunder Magic: Press Button A on Controller 2, then press and hold Left on Controller 1 and press Button B on Controller 2.

Increase Magic Level/Hit Points of Friend: Press Button A on Controller 2, then press and hold Right on Controller 1 and press Button B on Controller 2.

Increase Thunder Magic: Press Button A on Controller 2, then press and hold Button B on Controller 1 and press Button B on Controller 2.

Slow Mo

To pause the game for frame-by-frame slo' mo': Press Button A on Controller 2.

Tap repeatedly for frame-by-frame.

To deactivate slo' mo': Press Button B on Controller 2.

✳ Altered Beast ✳

Begin As Any Beast

Be a beast of a different color with this *Altered Beast* trick that enables you to begin as any creature. Before you turn on your Genesis, press and hold Down and Left on your control pad while simultaneously holding Buttons A, B, and C. Continue

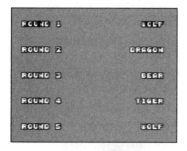

to hold these buttons and turn on your Genesis. When the Title screen appears, press Start. A Selection screen comes on-screen that enables you to select which altered ego you'd like to become in each round.

Pick Your Fight

Need a more beastly challenge? To select *Altered Beast*'s skill level, simply hold down Button B while you press Start and wait until the Title screen appears. A Play Select menu will appear that enables you to choose the game's challenge, number of lives you begin with, and the strength of your power meter.

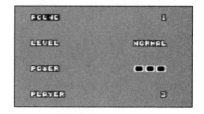

Continue

You can continue in *Altered Beast*. After you die, simply press and hold Button A and hit Start two times.

Sound Test

Grrr . . . To check out all of *Altered Beast*'s sounds, simultaneously press Buttons A, C, Right, Start, and Up on your control pad.

Score 100,000 Bonus Points

Use this strategy to score 100,000 Bonus Points in any round of *Altered Beast*. Kill the first, second, and third blue wolves that attack you. At the same time, try to grab all three Power-

Up balls that turn you into the Altered Beast. If you succeed you'll earn 100,000 Bonus Points when you destroy Neff at the end of the round. If you miss any of the Power-Up balls, Neff won't turn into the enemy boss right away. When you beat him, you'll earn only 50,000 instead of 100,000 points.

✂ Arcus Odyssey ✂

Journey out confidently with these passwords that give your characters all the strength they'll need for victory in *Arcus Odyssey*:

Jedda	Diana
Act 2: KDEEEBHDZC	**Act 2:** KDUEEBHDRS
Act 3: KGEUEEGHS2	**Act 3:** KGU2EEGHSU
Act 4: K4EEMWTIDQ	**Act 4:** KOUEUWLI1Q
Act 5: K4EEM4TPU3	**Act 5:** KOUEU4LPM3
Act 6: K4EEM4TTVC	**Act 6:** KOUEU4LTNC
Act 7: K4EEM4TXOH	**Act 7:** KOUEU4LXWH
Act 8: K4EEM4TZHM	**Act 8:** KOUEU4LZ5M

Erin	Bead
Act 2: KDMEEBHCZK	**Act 2:** JD2EEBHABZ
Act 3: KGMEEEGGSU	**Act 3:** JG2MEEGEKL
Act 4: K4MEEWLK1I	**Act 4:** 0G2EEOTI1Q
Act 5: K4MEE4TOU3	**Act 5:** 0G2EE4TP2F
Act 6: K4MEE4TSVC	**Act 6:** 0G2EE4LQFC
Act 7: K4MEE4TWOH	**Act 7:** 0G2EE4LU4H
Act 8: K4MEE4TYHM	**Act 8:** 0G2EE4L0XM

You can mix and match these passwords for a two-player game as long as both players use a password for the same act number.

♗ Arnold Palmer Golf ♗

Enter the Fantasy Zone

Take a break from the *Arnold Palmer Golf* scene with this far-out trick that transports you to the Fantasy Zone. To find it, begin a new game and then take 100 strokes on any hole without dropping the ball into the cup. The words "Game Over" will appear on-screen. Now,

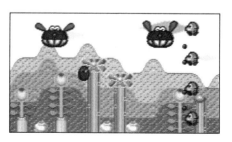

press Up, Up, Down, Down, Left, Right, Left, Right, and Button A on your control pad. Once you hit the Fantasy Zone, use Button B to shoot and Button C to drop bombs.

Secret Tournament

Grab your favorite knickers and use this special password to enter a secret *Arnold Palmer Golf* tournament with a very experienced caddy. Just enter lower case *f*'s all the way across the top row of the Password screen and 9's all the way across the bottom row.

Tournament Passwords

Tee off in different rounds of *Arnold Palmer Golf* with these swinging passwords:

Use this password to play a head-to-head match in Round 6. You're the champion with $340,000, Power 7, Skill 7, and Caddy Level 4:

> ElA+ CpJ0 KAFU 7BEU
> VAqC RGSW pk4E goL8
> LrHo

Here's a password that enables you to tee off in Round 8 as the tournament leader. You've got $348,000, Power 7, Skill 7, and Caddy Level 4:

> B1J- Pyo3 IIFA vUQ4
> aPCC RCao SU8E goUI
> a4TO

Tee off in Round 9 with this password. You have $358,000, Skill 8, Power 7, and Caddy Level 4:

> BhMu +TI- qCBR +g0L
> KdIK SWK5 W44A EIY7
> XxWa

This password puts you in Round 10, the second Match Play Round. You're a second tier winner with $372,000, Power 8, Skill 9, and Caddy Level 4:

> F1fp 5+D3 CCEE -08D
> KXIg TC6e GJIQ NJEQ
> RFXC

⚡ Back to the Future III ⚡

Level Skip

There's an easy way to skip back and forth through time in *Back to the Future III*. Begin a regular game, and then press Start to pause the action. Next, press and hold Button A and then press Up, Down,  Left, and Right on your control pad to advance a level. Repeat this trick each time you want to skip to a new level.

Skip Stages

Warp ahead to the future with this Stage-Select trick for *Back to the Future III*. To activate the trick, pause the game any time during play. Next, simultaneously press Up and Button A together, then Down and Button A together, then Left and Button A together, and then Right and Button A together.

 Batman

Cruise through the Batmobile Level

Here's a slick trick that'll enable you to cruise through the Gotham City street level of *Batman* with nary a scratch to the Batmobile. When the stage begins, drive to the upper left-hand corner of the screen. Remain there during the entire stage and keep Batman's hide, and the Batmobile, intact.

1-Up Loop

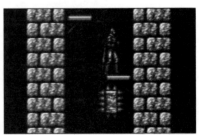

You'll be "batting" 1,000 with this 1-Up loop in Level 3 (The Flugelheim Museum) of *Batman*. When you reach the museum, grab the first 1-Up you reach. Next, jump on the moving platforms until you reach the ledge over the spiked object. Jump back down to the bottom moving platform. The 1-Up will reappear. Repeat this procedure until Batman's armed with nine Lives.

Another 1-Up Loop

Swoop to another 1-Up loop in Level 5 of *Batman*. When you reach the area where the clowns leap to the attack, go to the second platform with the first fire-breathing clown. Drop off the left side of the platform and you'll snag three 1-Ups as you fall. Keep at it until you've accumulated nine Lives.

Batarang Loop

You'll really drive the Joker "batty" if you grab 99 Batarangs in Level 3's Flugelheim Museum. When you reach the second elevator in the level, ride it to the top and defeat Axel. Jump and grab the Batarang icon. Now ride the elevator back down again. When you ride back up you'll find another Batarang icon. Repeat this procedure until you're armed with 99 Batarangs.

Another Batarang Loop

Do the Batarang loop one more time in Level 7-2 (The Cathedral) of *Batman*. In this level there's a Batman icon at the upper left of the screen just before you cross the first bridge you reach in the level. Grab this for five Batarangs. Next, jump down and then use your grappling hook to climb back up again. The

Batarang icon reappears. Repeat this procedure until you've grabbed 99 Batarangs. Now you're ready to zap the Joker.

✷ Batman: Revenge of the Joker ✷

The Ultimate Password

Same bat time, same bat channel. There's a super password that'll enable you to zap to any stage in *Batman: Revenge of the Joker*. Key in the code: 5257. After you've entered the code, a row of mushroom-like objects will appear across the bottom of the screen. Now, go to any stage by simply entering one of the following codes:

Stage 1-1:	1100	Stage 4 Boss:	4300
Stage 1-2:	1200	Stage 5-1:	5100
Stage 1 Boss:	1300	Stage 5-2:	5200
Stage 2-1:	2100	Stage 6-1:	6100
Stage 2-2:	2200	Stage 6-2:	6200
Stage 3-1:	3100	Stage 6 Boss:	6300
Stage 3-2:	3200	Stage 7-1:	7100
Stage 3 Boss:	3300	Final Battle	
Stage 4-1:	4100	with the Joker:	7200
Stage 4-2:	4200		

⚖ Beast Wrestler ⚖

Passwords!

Here are some monstrous *Beast Wrestler* passwords:

Beginner Rank
Match #2: MONSTERRQYQYQMQQQFAQQK
Match #3: MONSTERRQYQYQMQQQVAQSA
Match #4: MONSTERRAAQYQMWQIGAQSU
Match #5: MONSTERRZXAWADRDIUZQRM
Match #6: MONSTERRAAAWQMWQPBAQEF

World Rank

Match #1: MONSTERRAAAWQMWQPYAQKA

Match #2: MONSTERRAAAWADRDIHZQEF

Match #3: MONSTERRAAAWADRDINZQTN

Match #4: MONSTERRZXAWADRDIUZQRM

Match #5: MONSTERRZXAJADRDIJXQHI

Match #6: MONSTERRZXZXADRFDMXQBK

Match #7: MONSTERRZXZXADRFDIZQKX

Match #8: MONSTERRZXZXAJRTWKXQVX

Match #9: MONSTERRZXZXAJRTWOXQIH

Final Match Password

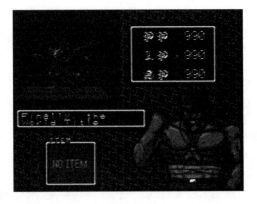

One more time, use this *Beast Wrestler* password to face off in the cart's grand finale:

BONILLARWIWIWIFYNOXQCD

Sound Test

Check out *Beast Wrestler*'s scary noises with this Sound Test. First, wait for the Title screen to appear. Then, simultaneously press and hold Buttons A, B,

and C, and press Start. The word "Test" should appear in the lower-left corner of the screen. Use Up and Down on your control pad to change the sounds and press Button A to select a sound. When you're done, press Button B to leave the screen.

⚖ Budokan ⚖

Exit Stage Right

If the *Budokan* bruisers turn your nose into eggplant, you can exit any match with ease. Simply press Buttons A, B, and C simultaneously and you're outta the action. The only down side—you'll lose the current match.

● Bulls vs. Lakers and the NBA Playoffs ●

Passwords:

Here are a few codes that'll enable you to slam dunk *Bulls vs. Lakers* playing against just about any team you like:

Play in the championship as the Bulls vs. the Lakers:	OXOBFBBC
Ending Ceremonies:	OXWBBBBD
Play in the championship as the Bulls vs. the Jazz:	NXOBBBBL
Ending Ceremonies:	NXWBBBBD
Play in the championship as the Bulls vs. the Supersonics:	MXOBFBBB
Ending Ceremonies:	MXWBBBBC
Play in the championship as the Lakers vs. the 76ers:	PLOBFBBB
Ending Ceremonies:	PLWBBBBC
Play in the championship as the Lakers vs. the Bucks:	BLOBFBBF
Ending Ceremonies:	BLWBBBBK
Play in the championship as the Lakers vs. the Bulls:	CLOBFBBC
Ending Ceremonies:	CLWBBBBF

**Play in the championship as
the 76ers vs. the Warriors:**   28OBFBBB
Ending Ceremonies: 28WBBBBB

**Play in the championship as
the 76ers vs. the Blazers:**   78OBFBBB
Ending Ceremonies: 78WBBBBB

**Play in the championship as
the 76ers vs. the Suns:**   68OBFBBB
Ending Ceremonies: 68WBBBBB

**Play in the championship as
the Jazz vs. the Pistons:**   LVOBFBBF
Ending Ceremonies: LVWBBBBJ

**Play in the championship as
the Jazz vs. the Hawks:**   MVOBFBBC
Ending Ceremonies: MVWBBBBF

**Play in the championship as
the Jazz vs. the Bucks:**   WVOBFBBC
Ending Ceremonies: WVWBBBBF

**Play in the championship as
the Celtics vs. the Blazers:**   HNOBFBBB
Ending Ceremonies: HNWBBBBC

**Play in the championship as
the Celtics vs. the Warriors:**   BNOBFBBC
Ending Ceremonies: BNWBBBBD

**Play in the championship as
the Celtics vs. the Rockets:**   MNOBFBBB
Ending Ceremonies: MNWBBBBC

**Play in the championship as the
Pistons vs. the Supersonics:**   NSOBFBBB
Ending Ceremonies: NSWBBBBB

**Play in the championship as
the Pistons vs. the Jazz:**   1SOBFBBB
Ending Ceremonies: 1SWBBBBB

**Play in the championship as
the Pistons vs. the Blazers:**   7SOBFBBB
Ending Ceremonies: 7SWBBBBB

**Play in the championship as
the Spurs vs. the Bucks:**   BGOBFBBD
Ending Ceremonies: BGWBBBBG

**Play in the championship as
the Spurs vs. the Bulls:**   FGOBFBBB
Ending Ceremonies: FGWBBBBC

**Play in the championship as
the Spurs vs. the Hawks:**   HGOBFBBC
Ending Ceremonies: HGWBBBBF

**Play in the championship as
the Bucks vs. the Suns:**   HDOBFBBB
Ending Ceremonies: HDWBBBBC

**Play in the championship as
the Bucks vs. the Blazers:**   CDOBFBBB
Ending Ceremonies: CDWBBBBC

**Play in the championship as
the Bucks vs. the Spurs:**   FDOBFBBB
Ending Ceremonies: FDWBBBBB

**Play in the championship as
the Hawks vs. the Lakers:**   54OBFBBB
Ending Ceremonies: 54WBBBBB

**Play in the championship as
the Hawks vs. the Spurs:**   24OBFBBC
Ending Ceremonies: 24WBBBBD

**Play in the championship as
the Hawks vs. the Rockets:**   64OBFBBC
Ending Ceremonies: 64WBBBBD

**Play in the championship as
the Knicks vs. the Lakers:**   HJOBFBBB
Ending Ceremonies: HJWBBBBB

**Play in the championship as
the Knicks vs. the Suns:**   KJOBFBBB
Ending Ceremonies: KJWBBBBB

**Play in the championship as
the Knicks vs. the Warriors:**   BJOBFBBB
Ending Ceremonies: BJWBBBBC

**Play in the championship as the
Supersonics vs. the Bucks:**   BQOBFBBD
Ending Ceremonies: BQWBBBBH

**Play in the championship as the
Supersonics vs. the 76ers:**   MQOBFBBC
Ending Ceremonies: MQWBBBBD

**Play in the championship as
the Warriors vs. the Bucks:**   P6WBBBBC
Ending Ceremonies: P6WBBBBC

**Play in the championship as
the Warriors vs. the 76ers:**   56OBFBBB
Ending Ceremonies: 56WBBBBC

**Play in the championship as
the Warriors vs. the Hawks:**   M6OBFBBC
Ending Ceremonies: M6WBBBBD

**Play in the championship as
the Rockets vs. the Hawks:**   M2OBFBBC
Ending Ceremonies: M2WBBBBF

**Play in the championship as
the Rockets vs. the Pacers:**   T2OBFBBB
Ending Ceremonies: T2WBBBBB

**Play in the championship as
the Rockets vs. the Pistons:**   Q2OBFBBB
Ending Ceremonies: Q2WBBBBJ

**Play in the championship as the
Pacers vs. the Supersonics:**   NOOBFBBB
Ending Ceremonies: NOWBBBBC

**Play in the championship as
the Pacers vs. the Lakers:**   COOBFBBB
Ending Ceremonies: COWBBBBB

Play in the championship as	
the Pacers vs. the Rockets:	GOOBFBBB
Ending Ceremonies:	GOWBBBBC
Play in the championship as	
the Blazers vs. the Bulls:	KBOBFBBB
Ending Ceremonies:	KBWBBBBB
Play in the championship as	
the Blazers vs. the Celtics:	7BOBFBBC
Ending Ceremonies:	7BWBBBBD
Play in the championship as	
the Blazers vs. the 76ers:	MBOBFBBC
Ending Ceremonies:	MBWBBBBF
Play in the championship as	
the Suns vs. the 76ers:	PZOBFBBB
Ending Ceremonies:	PZWBBBBC
Play in the championship as	
the Suns vs. the Celtics:	LZOBFBBD
Ending Ceremonies:	LZWBBBBG
Play in the championship as	
the Suns vs. the Bulls:	FZOBFBBB
Ending Ceremonies:	FZWBBBBC

Passwords

Play as the Bulls all the way through the playoffs:

First Round: Bulls vs. Celtics,	
Game 7 (series tied):	WXVBQCVL
Second Round: Bulls vs. Cavs,	
Game 4 (Bulls lead, 3-0):	WXZBQJBD
Third Round: Bulls vs. Knicks,	
Game 4 (Bulls lead, 3-0):	WXXBQ2BK
Finals: Bulls vs. Warriors,	
Game 4 (Bulls lead, 3-0):	WXOBTBBC
Championship Trophy	
Presentation:	WXWBQBBC

✦ Burning Force ✦

10 Lives per Continue

Set the screen on fire in *Burning Force* with this trick that enables you to begin with 10 Lives per Continue. Wait until

the Title screen appears and then press Start. When the words "Start/Option" appear on-screen, press Button B, Button A, Button B, Button A two times, Button C, Button A two times, and Start on your control pad. Now, feel the heat!

Castle of Illusion
☆ Starring Mickey Mouse ☆

Earn Tons of Lives

Oh no! Here's a slow, but sure way to max out your Lives in *Castle of Illusion Starring Mickey Mouse*. All you have to do is jump onto the second swinging vine in Level 1-1 of the game. You can hang there and swing back and forth,

hitting butterflies for as long as you like. Unfortunately, it takes an hour to collect enough points to earn two Lives! But, hey, just leave the game on and come back later.

End of Level 1-Up

Mickey's small, but he's mighty. At the end of any level, wait until the Bonus Point Add-up screen appears, and then rapidly tap Start until you hear a ringing sound. This gives you a 1-Up!

More Lives for Mickey

Level 2-2's another area in *Castle of Illusion* where you can max out your Lives. You'll find a Jack-in-the-Box marked with a question mark just before you exit the stage. Bounce on the clown that pops out of the box and then walk left to grab special items and 1,000 points. Next, return to the question mark. You can repeat this procedure as many times as you like. You'll earn an Extra Life with every 50,000 points.

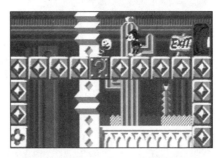

Secret Rooms

Mickey's got a secret, actually quite a few secrets. Check out these hidden rooms in *Castle of Illusion*.

The Enchanted Forest

Round 1, Level 2: Fall into the left side of the fifth hole you reach. Jump to the ledge on the right for a special item bag.

Round 1, Level 4: Jump into the hole to the left of the tall tree laden with special items. You'll find more special items in the hole.

Toyland

Round 2, Level 2: From the beginning of the level, go right and jump on the spring. Move left until you reach another spring. Vault to the upper section. Move right until you reach the end of this area and then jump, holding Right on 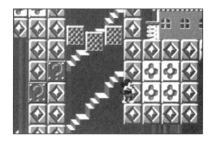 your control pad. This takes you straight to the door of another secret room filled with special items.

The Storm

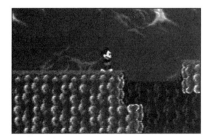
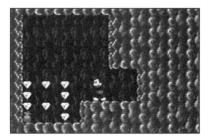

Round 3, Level 1: Jump into the first hole you reach and walk left.

The Library

Round 4, Level 2: From the beginning of the level, move left and leap to the ledge. Using the chain, continue to your left, and then head up. Run to the right, past the falling books, and then go up and to the left. When you reach the tea cup, jump inside for a surprise. Next, continue to the right. When you reach the area where you have to jump, hold Right on your control pad. You'll land near another secret room with a black door. Finally, run to the right of the apple and down the hill. When you reach a cup of tea, jump inside for another secret room!

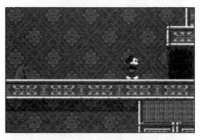

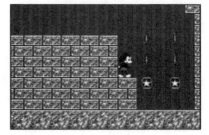

The Castle

Round 5, Level 1: Jump into the second hole and then jump up and to the right to reach a secret room. Continue in this

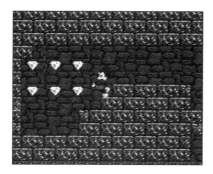

level until you reach the area with the large rolling rock. Fall into the third hole, duck to avoid the rock, and then proceed up and left to find a secret area.

○ Centurion: Defender of Rome ○

World-Bending Passwords

Stand firm, Caesar wannabes! Here are some cool *Centurion: Defender of Rome* passwords:

Six Cavalry/Hispania, Narbonensis, Italia, Gaul, Alpes, Germania, Sicilia, Dalmatia. Rank: General.

GS4A LK1I RA6Q JESV L55U CXGA

One Consular, Seven Cavalry/Hispania, Narbonensis, Gaul, Alpes, Italia, Sicilia, Dalmatia, Germania, Dacia, Thracis, Macedonia. Rank: Consul.

INJQ P717 TEPQ JGSV K15W JXXB

Twelve Consular/Hispania, Narbonensis, Gaul, Alpes, Germania, Italia, Sicilia, Dalmatia, Dacia, Thracia, Macedonia, Mesopotamia, Armenia, Arabia, Aegyptus. Rank: ProConsul.

QBRA TLUZ XAPT ZHVK VLVB TN7A

Twelve Consular/The entire world except: Britannia, Sardinia, Sarmatia, Scythia, Parthia, Mesopotamia, Carthago, Mauretania. Rank: ProConsul.

QL7A SY55 XP5W ZHNK VKVB PAYG

Twelve Consular/The entire world except: Parthia, Scythia.

MN6A QJBC 5P55 5PNK VKXS SV61

Rule the World

Strap on your sandals. Here's the ultimate password for *Centurion: Defender of Rome:*

QDUA YQ25 5555
55NK VKXW IPJI

(Enter the password and then go to Italia and select "Tribute Policy" and then " ". Next, go to the Map screen and keep selecting "End Turn." Eventually, the game will end and you'll win!)

⚔ Chakan the Forever Man ⚔

Here's an eternal trick that'll give Chakan all the weapons he needs. Choose the Practice mode and then begin play. Stand on the little platform just above the sky portal and press Start. Use the Passage spell. You'll vault forward 12 levels and be stoked with all the weapons you can use.

▥ Columns ▥

Instant Magic Jewel

When the odds are stacked against you in *Columns*, use this trick to make a Magic Jewel appear whenever you need it. Play the Arcade mode on the Easy setting. When you begin to lose, stack the jewels on the far-left and far-right sides of the column as high as possible. When the piles are stacked as high as they can go, the Magic Jewel will appear.

○ Cool Spot ○

Level Select

Wait until you Spot this level select code. Any time during the game, press Button A, Button B, Button C, Button B, Button A, Button C, Button A, Button B,

Button C, Button B, Button A, and Button C. If you performed the trick correctly, you'll hear a tone, and then the Level Completed screen appears. You're on to the next level.

❄ Cyberball ❄

Super Passwords!

Yee haw! Use these codes to go undefeated all the way to the playoffs as the Dallas Destroyers:

1 win:	LBBB B7CB BDVV
2 wins:	LVBB BB9B BDXV
3 wins:	LXBB B7LB BD3B
4 wins:	LIBB B8FB BDTV
5 wins:	LLBB B7DB BDNB
6 wins:	LKBB BBBV BDCV
7 wins:	LMBB BLCV BD2V
8 wins:	LOBB BLPB BFHV
9 wins:	LFBB BLHB BD8B
10 wins:	LCBB BFOV BDKX
11 wins:	L7BB BXGB BDRV
12 wins:	L4BB BF2B BDAV
13 wins:	LRBB BFVV BDTV
14 wins:	LTBB BFCX BD2V
15 wins:	L8BB BFJI BDMX
16 wins:	LZBB BR2S IDKI
Playoff One:	LUBB BRHV BDZV
Playoff Two:	L5BB BXUV BD2V

Special Strategies

Use these tricks of the *Cyberball* trade to score big.

On offense, run the following four plays for easy scores:

1. **Axle Grind:** Throw left to the wide receiver for a quick TD.
2. **Sunday Ride:** To cross the 50 yard line for some quick yardage, throw left to the running back.
3. **Zig-Zag:** To score inside the 10 yard line, or just chew up some easy turf, toss the ball to the left running back.
4. **Suicide:** To score inside the 10 yard line or score extra points after TD's, throw to the left running back.

On defense, use these primo plays to stop the computer with negative yardage and score lots of safeties.

1. **Prevent:** For the sack, blitz your linebacker around the left side of the offensive line.
2. **3-4 Defense:** When the computer is inside your 10 yard line, blitz your linebacker around either side. Use your power booster to nail the QB.

Kickoff TD Trick

You'll get a kick out of this easy score kick return in *Cyberball.* Grab the ball after a kickoff. Now run between the two defenders on the right and then dash up the sideline. Do it right and you'll rack up the TDs!

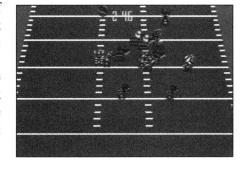

• David Robinson's Supreme Court •

Passwords

Here are a few bouncy passwords that'll put David Robin-
son on court in a big way:

> **Most Valuable Player:**
> IIDSREQUS
>
> **Championship:**
> IIDSREQ3R

✳ Deadly Moves ✳

Passwords

Here are some killer passwords for *Deadly Moves*:

Level 3: V3A 5FTQ NHG
Level 4: V3A MFDK 01A
Level 5: HBV MFD3 25H
Level 6: IY5 MFD4 046
Level 7: EVV ZFDG QMD

☆ DecapAttack ☆

Score Tons of 1-Ups

Don't lose your head over *DecapAttack*. Here's a surefire way to load up on 1-Ups. Once you've collected all five coins, place them in the channel listed below for each bonus round:

> **Bonus Round 1:** Channel 2 (from left)
> **Bonus Round 2:** Channel 5 (from left)
> **Bonus Round 3:** Channel 3 (from left)
> **Bonus Round 4:** Channel 5 (from left)

Put each of your five guys in the channels and when they reach the top, press Button C as rapidly as possible. Now you'll win big!

Extra Energy

Use your head to find this energy boost in *DecapAttack*. First, hunt for a spring pole. When you reach the pole, jump and land on top of it, use the Airwalk technique—press Button C rapidly after you  jump. If you do this correctly you'll hear a sound that indicates you've earned an Extra Life, and a red band on the pole will turn white. You can repeat this procedure over and over until you run out of red bands on the pole.

Bypass Toady

If you're not in the mood for a fight, there's an easy way to skip Round 2's boss, Toady, in *DecapAttack*. When you reach the last drop just before Toady, use Airwalk to float to the ledge on the left. Jump from ledge to ledge and before you know it you'll clear the round. Psst . . . don't forget to get the special item before you leave Round 2 or you'll have to return later.

☜ Desert Strike: Return to the Gulf ☜

Just for Fun

Just for kicks, try to destroy the *Desert Strike* Title screen. Wait until the words "Desert Strike" appear on the Title screen, and then press Button A to launch missiles from the helicopter.

Five Lives Password

Power-up with five fightin' Lives before you begin your attack in *Desert Strike*. All you have to do is enter this simple password: TQQQLOM. You can also punch in this code before you enter your Mission password.

Passwords Galore

Return to the Gulf again and again with these *Desert Strike* passwords:

> **Mission 2:** TQOHLOX
> **Mission 3:** KLJHTOI
> **Mission 4:** BEFIKLN

○ **Devilish** ○

Begin with 99 Balls

Here's a bouncy trick that'll give you 99 balls at the beginning of *Devilish*. Just wait until the Title screen appears, and then simultaneously press and hold Buttons A, B, C, and Left.

☆ **DinoLand** ☆

Level Select

Return to the past and choose any level in *DinoLand*. Pause your game, and then press Down, Up, and Down six times. Next, press Down, Up, and Down six more times. Finally, simultaneously press Button B and Start. When your game begins, simply press Button A to zap to another level.

Bonus Points and Sky World Warp

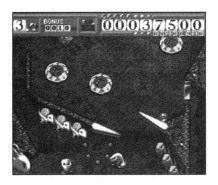

If you're handy with your paddle, you can pull off some surprises in *DinoLand*. First off, try to launch the ball and catch it on your paddle. Next, bump the machine 23 times with Button B. Now, shoot for the slot machine without bumping the machine again. If your aim is true, you'll win

a free ball and 100,000 Bonus Points. Don't stop now! If you can bump the machine 23 more times and then hit the slot machine again, you'll warp to Sky World. Repeat this procedure six more times or so and you'll snag an extra million points!

✳ Disney's Aladdin ✳

Level Skip

You won't need three wishes when you plug in this easy level skip trick for *Disney's Aladdin*. When you want to skip levels, just press Start to pause the game. Then press A, B, B, A, A, B, B, and then A. You can repeat this trick as many times as you like until you reach the level of your choice.

♨ Dragon's Fury ♨

Password

Plug in this fire-breathing password to begin with 13 million points and 99 balls:

UFELFO78TL

Music Select

Tired of the tunes? Use the password to change the music:

OMAKEBGM01

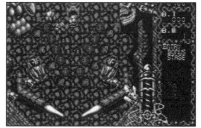

Change the final digit of the password to change the tunes. Use the numbers 0-4.

Final Password

Enter this password to skip straight to the end of *Dragon's Fury*:

6RENAXUEMW

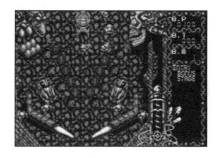

✸ Dynamite Duke ✸

Secret Option Screen

Here's an explosive trick that enables you to access a secret Option mode in *Dynamite Duke*. Enter the Option mode, press Button C ten times, and then press Start. Now you can skip stages, add Extra Lives, and even boost your Continues.

```
     SUPER OPTIONS

 ▸ GAME LEVEL  EASY
   BGM          01
   EFFECT       01
   MISSION      01
   LIFE         03
   CONTINUE     05
   D PANCH      05
   EXIT
```

✦ Earnest Evans ✦

Stage Skip

Whip yourself into *Earnest Evans* action with this stage-skipping code. Whenever you're ready to skip a stage, pause the game. Next, press Up, Button A, Down, Button B, Left, Button A, Right, Button B, and then un-pause. Voilà!

⋈ Ecco the Dolphin ⋈

Passwords

Ecco can swim straight to any area in the game with these passwords:

The Undercaves:	UYNAINCC
The Vents:	FKWLACCA
The Lagoon:	NDRBRIKR
Ridge Water:	HYAUGFLV
Open Ocean:	FNCQWBMT
Ice Zone:	DWFFZBMV
Hard Water:	QGDJRQLA
Cold Water:	MCLFRQLW
Jurassic Beach:	PLABUNLT
Pteranadon Pond:	FQREUNLI
Origin Beach:	QXKIUNLX
Island Zone:	UWXIOQLK
Deep Water:	EILQOQLC
The Marble Sea:	XAKUQQLS
The Library:	FDGXQQLC
Deep City:	ZUVPQQLU
City of Forever:	AABBRQLU
Trilobite Circle:	OBEMUNLX
Dark Water:	JNXPUNLA
City of Forever:	ZBPIGPLD
The Tube:	KUVEKMLK
Welcome to the Machine:	SDDBKMLG
The Last Fight:	KNLMLMLC

Air Passwords

If you're having trouble keeping Ecco alive, try plugging in one of these unlimited air codes:

The Undercaves:	LEVELSCT
The Lagoon:	SHARKFIN
Cold Water:	LNXHXRLB
Deep Water:	OEWSURLC
The Tube:	FIVEPODS
The Machine:	ECCOFMLY

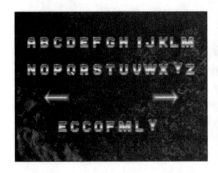
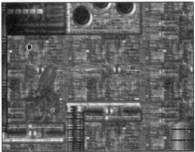

Passwords: Just for Fun

Enter this weird password (the name of the former Sega guru, Al Nilsen) as your password to go directly to the last fight. The password is: ALNELSIN.

Ultimate Password

Here's a password that enables you to begin *Ecco the Dolphin* without any air meter, which means you've got all the air you need in any level. The password is: LIFEFISH.

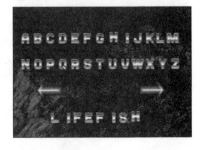

Stop the Music

Use this trick to hear Ecco splash through the briny deep with sound effects, but no music. Any time during your game, press Start to pause. Then, press Button A five times. Press Start again to resume play and enjoy the sounds of the sea.

Invincibility

With a flip of the fin (and this super simple pad trick) Ecco can become invincible. Go to the Password screen, enter any password, and then press and hold Button A and press Start until the game begins. Press Start to unpause, and you'll discover you're completely invincible.

♨ El Viento ♨

Color Test

No, you're not hallucinating. You can make a weird Color Test bar appear in *El Viento*. All you have to do is wait for the Wolf Team logo to appear on-screen,

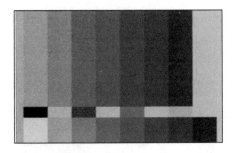

and then simultaneously press Buttons A, B, and C, and then press Start. This Color Test is just for fun.

Skip Stages

Skip a stage, any stage, in *El Viento*. To activate the trick, pause your game during play. Press Up, Left, Right, Down, and Button B on your control pad and you're off and running on the next level! Repeat this procedure for each stage you wish to skip.

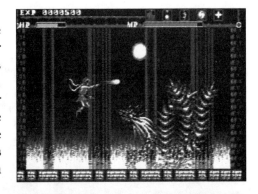

Magic Power-Up

Magic anyone? Here's a trick that'll charge up your magic abilities in *El Viento*. Pause the game any time during play. Next, press Up, Left, Right, Down, and

Button C for each additional magic ability you wish to learn.

Slow Motion

Put it into low gear in *El Viento* with this slo' mo' trick. Hit Start to pause your game any time during play. Next, press Up, Left, Right, Down, and Button A. Now, push any key and you're in slow motion.

☆ **E-SWAT** ☆

Sound Test

You can hear all of *E-SWAT*'s sounds, but first you have to beat the game! When you reach the ending scene, simultaneously press Buttons A, B, C, Down, and Left on your control pad. While still holding all of these buttons, press Start repeatedly until the Sound Select screen appears.

Evander Holyfield's "Real Deal" Boxing

Password

This monstrous code puts you behind the gloves as a strange green boxer who packs maximum punch. When the Title screen appears, choose Career mode and then select Start New Career. Name your fighter "The Beast," press Start, and the fun begins.

Win the Easy Way

Even though the Beast is tough, he can win without having to fight at all. After you've used the Beast trick, wait for the crowd to cheer as the Beast raises his hand at the beginning of a bout. As the camera scans the ring, wait until it's not pointing at either boxer, and then press Start and quit the bout. When the Training screen appears, you'll discover you got the win! The only catch is, this drains your fighter's energy somewhat, so train up before the next fight.

❊ Ex-Mutants ❊

Special Options Screen

Use this ex-cellent code to give your Mutants a bunch of special options. When the Title screen appears, select the Options screen. Set the Music to "05" and the Sound FX to "21." Move the cursor to "Exit," then simultaneously press Buttons A, B, C, and Start. If you've performed the trick correctly, Shannon will say "Too Easy," and the Cheater Mode menu will appear. You can pick any of the different options, including a stage select, maximum Lives, or unlimited weapons.

✦ F-22 Interceptor ✦

Passwords!!

It's high flying for *F-22* pilots with these passwords for the entire game!

United States	Iraq
Mission 1: 0HG02I	**Mission 1:** C6G022
Mission 2: 0PG06D	**Mission 2:** CEG06L
Mission 3: 0TG0E0	**Mission 3:** CIG0A4
Mission 4: 11G0I2	**Mission 4:** CM60EC
Mission 5: 15G0MA	**Mission 5:** CUG0IO
Mission 6: 19G0UM	**Mission 6:** D2G0U2
Mission 7: 1DG163	**Mission 7:** D6O1EV
Mission 8: 1LG1EQ	**Mission 8:** DAO1QM
Mission 9: 1PG1M6	**Mission 9:** DQG2EJ
Mission 10: 1TG1UI	**Mission 10:** E2G3AI
Mission 11: 21G26I	**Mission 11:** E6G428
Mission 12: 2TG32I	**Mission 12:** EAG5E7
Mission 13: 31G3UJ	**Mission 13:** EEG5UR
Mission 14: 35G4A4	**Mission 14:** EIG6QS
Mission 15: 39G56U	**Mission 15:** EUG7MS
Mission 16: 3TG5IC	**Mission 16:** F2G7UB
Mission 17: 41G62K	**Mission 17:** F6G8AS
Mission 18: 45G6MJ	**Mission 18:** FAG8UR
Mission 19: 4TG7A7	**Mission 19:** FEGAIS
Mission 20: 5167QL	**Mission 20:** FIKB6I
Mission 21: 59G8EI	**Mission 21:** FQGBUL
Mission 22: 61Q9EM	**Mission 22:** FUGCEA
Mission 23: 65Q9QA	**Mission 23:** G2GDQL
Mission 24: 69Q9QA	**Mission 24:** G6UF6E
Mission 25: 6HG9UJ	**Mission 25:** GIUFU0
Mission 26: 6LGAIJ	**Mission 26:** GMUHAI

Korea

Mission 1: 7E002E

Mission 2: 7M006Q

Mission 3: 7Q01AA

Mission 4: 8201QS

Mission 5: 8601U4

Mission 6: 8A022D

Mission 7: 8I02E8

Mission 8: 8M042R

Mission 9: 8Q04MQ

Mission 10: 8U05MV

Mission 11: 9A05UK

Mission 12: 9I06A9

Mission 13: 9U06U9

Mission 14: A2072C

Mission 15: A608E4

Mission 16: AA08IJ

Mission 17: AE08U3

Mission 18: AIF9UU

Mission 19: AMFB6C

Mission 20: B20B47

Mission 21: B60BMN

Mission 22: BAFCIL

Russia

Mission 1: HJ0024

Mission 2: HR412H

Mission 3: I701QI

Mission 4: IB02EI

Mission 5: IF02U6

Mission 6: IJE4EH

Mission 7: INE567

Mission 8: IRE6AN

Mission 9: J306QK

Mission 10: J707UT

Mission 11: JF08M5

Mission 12: JJ096J

Mission 13: JNE9Q7

Mission 14: JREA2K

Mission 15: JVEBMK

Mission 16: KB0CA1

Mission 17: KF0D2N

Mission 18: KJ0DUU

Mission 19: KN0EIN

The Aces Challenge

Mission 1: LJG02V

Mission 2: LNG067

Mission 3: LRG0AM

Mission 4: LVG0EU

Mission 5: M3G0I0

Mission 6: M7G0UG

Mission 7: MBG16T

Mission 8: MFG1EG

Mission 9: MJG1MS

☀ Faery Tale Adventure ☀

Power Up with Special Items

Here's a "faerly" easy trick that enables you to quickly grab tons of treasure in *Faery Tale Adventure*. Save your game just before you open a treasure chest. Next, open the treasure chest and gather the goodies. Now save your game again. When you return to the saved game, you'll find you reappear just in front of the same treasure chest again — and it's been refilled with loot. Repeat this procedure until you've amassed mucho goodies from any treasure chest.

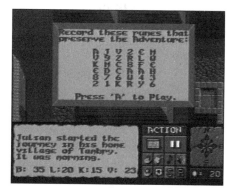

Super Power Password

It will be a *Faery Tale Adventure* when you begin with this mega-power password. You'll begin at Tambry's Tavern with plenty of items plus a sword:

BJ22JZ
EHZXWR
KXF8HE
896A77
T7FG43
J7KRE7

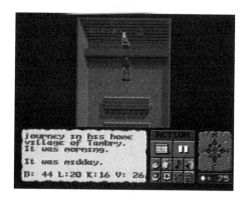

★ Fantasia ★

Easy Power-Up!

Bouncing on different creatures often makes special items appear in *Fantasia*. To snag Power-Ups right at the beginning of the game, wait until the first Broom that dances along the bottom of the screen reaches the stairs. Bounce on it, and three Crystal Balls, two Stars, and a Magic Book will appear.

Secret Room

Teach Mickey to lurk in the shadows and he'll find a secret bonus room in the second part of the Castle. Stand in front of this shadow and you'll zap to the secret room. Inside are four Stars and two Magic Books.

1-Up Loop

Fantasia's a Mickey Mouse game if you use this 1-Up loop in World 1-2 to max out your Lives. Near the beginning of the level you'll reach a series of platforms, the top of which has a musical note on it that

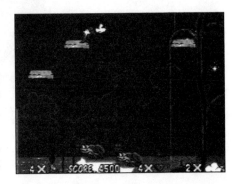

gives you a 1-Up. Once you've grabbed the note, continue until you reach a treasure chest. If you jump into the chest you'll warp back to the beginning of the level. Repeat this procedure, grabbing the note each time, until you have nine Lives.

Another 1-Up Loop

No, it's not a fantasy. There is another 1-Up loop in *Fantasia*. This one's in the Earth World. Proceed through the level until you reach the first Fairy.

Inside the Crystal Cave, jump to the first platform you reach and grab the Note 1-Up.

Keep moving through the cave and grab the Note just past the two boulders.

Grab the third Note just before you reach the Fairy, but don't touch the Fairy.

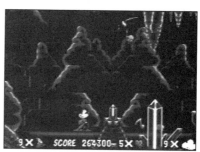

Instead, let yourself die and collect all three 1-Ups again. You can continue to repeat this process until you've maxed out your Lives. Psst . . . this same trick works in the Desert World.

Max Out Your Items

You can leave any area in *Fantasia* and return to find that all the special items have reappeared. For example, in the Air World, you can go through the Pastorale again and again to snag Notes.

✕ Fighting Masters ✕

There are two extra difficulty levels in *Fighting Masters*, but you need to use a special trick to access them. To reach the easiest level, go to the game's Options screen, and set the Level Select on "Easy," and Continue on "5." Then, go to the Music Select and listen to sound 8C, then 8B, and then 8A.

Next, go to Sound Select and listen to sound 90. To reach an especially difficult level, called Mania, follow the same procedure, but set the Level Select to "Hard."

 Flashback

Passwords

No more *Flashback* when you tackle any level of the game at any difficulty setting with this complete set of passwords:

Easy
Level 1: PIXEL
Level 2: BETSY
Level 3: PANCHO
Level 4: STUDIO
Level 5: TOHO
Level 6: AKANE
Level 7: INCBIN

Normal
Level 1: FALCON
Level 2: DATA
Level 3: MILORD
Level 4: QUICKEY
Level 5: BIJOU
Level 6: BUBBLE
Level 7: CLIP

Expert
Level 1: CLIO
Level 2: ACRTC
Level 3: BLUB
Level 4: STUN
Level 5: MIMOLO
Level 6: HECTOR
Level 7: KALIMA
Ending Code: CYGNUS

☆ Flicky ☆

A Bikini Babe

If you're faster than lightning at *Flicky*, the game may have a surprise in store for you. Complete the first 10 rounds in under 20 seconds each and get a perfect score in each bonus round. You should have just over 240,000 points. While you're awarded your Bonus, a window will open in the lower-left corner of the screen and a scantily clad girl in a bikini appears.

● The Flintstones ●

Level Select

Flintstones, meet the Flintstones . . . in fact, meet them anywhere you like with this Level Select code. When the Title screen appears, simultaneously press Buttons A, B, C, and Left. Continue to hold all of these buttons, and then press Start. Use Up and Down on your directional pad to choose any stage you like.

⊕ Forgotten Worlds ⊕

Continue

In case it's slipped your mind, you can't really continue in a one-player game of *Forgotten Worlds*, but there is a way to extend the action. Have Controller 2 plugged in and ready to go. When Player One's life meter drops close to zero, abandon him and rev up Player Two. You can continue with the same weapon. When Player Two is ready to drop, crank up Player One. Repeat this trick as many times as you like.

★ Gaiares ★

Configuration Mode

To check out the Configuration mode in *Gaiares*, just press and hold any button and then press Start. Note: You must release the other button the second you hit Start or the Configuration mode won't appear on-screen.

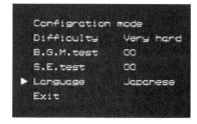

You can use this mode to select the difficulty of your game, listen to background music and sound effects, and even choose the C.M. language. Hey, you can even change everything to Japanese!

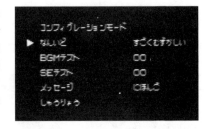

Stage Select

Tired of dying in Stage 1? Check out some higher stages via this slick trick for *Gaiares*. Go to the Configuration mode (see the previous section).

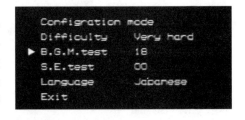

Next, select 18 on B.G.M. Now, press and hold Button A on

Controller 2 and exit the Configuration mode. A Stage Select screen will appear when your game begins.

Invincibility

Soar into space completely invincible with this trick for *Gaiares*. During play, pause the game and then simultaneously press and hold Buttons A, C, and Left. If you performed the trick correctly, the screen will freeze temporarily. You have to repeat this trick for each level.

Instant Weapon Power-Up

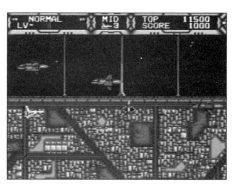

Use this trick to instantly power up your TOZ in *Gaiares*. First, use the Stage Select trick (see left). Now, any time during your game, pause and then press and hold Up and hit Button A twice. Next, un-pause your game and fire your TOZ to receive full power. You'll be zap-happy!

Choose Your Weapon

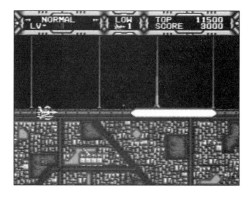

Pick a weapon, any weapon, with this trick that enables you to choose any weapon in *Gaiares*. To begin, perform the Stage Select trick (see left). Next, any time during your game, pause and then press and hold Up and press Button A. Each time you hit Button A you'll choose a different weapon. When you're armed with your weapon of choice, un-pause and fire away.

Secret Weapon!

There's an easy way to receive a special super-charged weapon, called the T-Braster, in *Gaiares*. All you have to do is fire your TOZ six times without hitting any enemies!

✳ Gain Ground ✳

Round Select

If you're feeling up in the air, use this Level Select trick for Gain Ground to put yourself back on track.

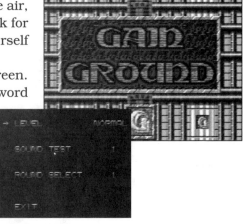

Go to the Option screen. Move the cursor to the word "Level." Next, press Button A, Button C, Button B, and Button C. The words "Round Select" will appear underneath "Sound Test."

✂ Galahad ✂

Infinite Lives and Level Skip

Be a knight in shining armor the easy way. Go to the game's Option screen and then enter a password if you have one (don't worry if you don't — the trick will still work). Next, enter

the password: LTUS. Begin your game and you'll discover that you have unlimited Lives. To skip levels, simultaneously press Start and Button A.

★ Galaxy Force 2 ★

Check Out the Endings

Skip straight to the ending sequences of *Galaxy Force 2* with this easy trick. Plug in both controllers. Enter the game's Option screen and highlight "Exit." Press

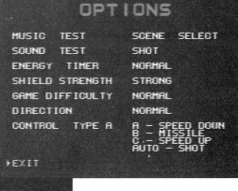

and hold Start on Controller 2, and then press Start on Controller 1. Now, prepare to get out of *Galaxy Force 2*'s world.

♟ Ghostbusters ♟

Rack Up the Cash

Don't get slimed! There's an easy way to collect tons of cash in *Ghostbusters*. Look for a safe that contains money and is close

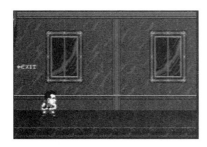

to the entrance of a maze. Grab the safe and leave the maze. Return to the maze and you'll find the safe—and the money—are back! Repeat this procedure until you have all the cash you want.

Ghouls 'n Ghosts

Level Select

The good news is that there's a Level Select trick for *Ghouls 'n Ghosts*. The bad news is that this trick only works with some *Ghouls 'n Ghosts* cartridges. You may have to try it several times to discover whether or not it works with your copy. To test the trick, press the directional button on your control pad Up, Down, Left, and then Right during the Title screen. Next, use one of the following pad combinations to reach your desired level:

Level 1

The Execution Place: Push Start.

The Floating Island on the Lake: Push Button A and Start simultaneously.

Level 2

The Village of Decay: Push Up, Button B, and Start simultaneously.

Town of Fire: Push Up, Button A, and Start simultaneously.

Level 3

Baron Rankle's Tower: Push Down, Button B, and Start simultaneously.

Horrible Faced Mountain: Push Down, Button A, and Start simultaneously.

Level 4

The Crystal Forest: Push Left, Button B, and Start simultaneously.

The Ice Slopes: Push Left, Button A, and Start simultaneously.

Level 5

Beginning of Castle: Push Right, Button B, and Start simultaneously.

Second Half of Castle: Push Right, Button B, and Start simultaneously.

Loki: Push Down/Right, Button A, and Start simultaneously.

Invincibility

If Sir Arthur's catching a cold from running around without his armor, we recommend you use this trick to become invincible—but remember that, just as with the Level Select trick, it only works with some *Ghouls 'n Ghosts* cartridges. Turn on your Genesis and then press Reset four times. Now, when the Title screen appears, press Button A four times. Next, press Up, Down, Left, and Right on your directional pad. If you've executed the trick correctly, you'll hear a tone. Next, hit Start to reach the Player Selection screen. Press and hold Button B and hit Start to begin the game. Continue to hold Button B while you play, and Arthur will be invincible!

More Invincibility

If the above Invincibility trick was a no-go, check this one out. Wait until the Title screen appears and then press Button A and Up together, then Button A and Down together, then Button A and Left together, then Button A and Right together, then hold Button B and press Start, then hold Button C and press Start. It's tough to make it work—just keep trying!

Slow Motion Code

Sir Arthur looks pretty cool in slo' mo', but just as with the invincibility and Level Select codes, this trick only works with some *Ghouls 'n Ghosts* cartridges. Wait until the Title screen appears, and then press Up, Button A, Down, Button A, Left, Button A, and Right. If you've done the trick correctly you'll hear a musical note at this point. Next, press Right and hit Start repeatedly until Sir Arthur appears. Now, press Start to pause the game and press and hold Button B. Continue to hold Button B and Arthur's in slo' mo'.

Nice Catch Message

It seems you *can* teach an old knight new tricks. If Sir Arthur grabs the Key that appears at the end of each stage of *Ghouls 'n Ghosts* he'll be rewarded with the message, "Nice Catch." To catch the Key stand to its right, close, but not too close, and leap to the left. The timing of this is quite tricky, but if you manage to grab the Key you'll see the message and earn a Bonus of 5,000 points.

Climb the Mystery Ladder

Here's a "just for fun" trick in the first level of *Ghouls 'n Ghosts*. Climb the second ladder you reach in Level 1. When you reach the top of the ladder stand in the center, jump straight up, and rapidly hit Left and Right on your controller. Now climb some more — you'll walk on air. It's gotta be the shoes!

⚖ Gods ⚖

Passwords

You won't need to be omniscient after you plug in these *Gods* passwords:

> **Level 1:** NASHWAN
> **Level 2:** COYOTE
> **Level 3:** FOXX

⚔ Golden Axe ⚔

Begin with 15 Lives

Take a hack at *Golden Axe* with 15 men. Select a two-player game, and immediately let one of your characters die. Now you can use either character as if you were playing a one-player game. This gives you three Lives plus four credits left, for a total of 15 spare soldiers!

Begin with up to 30 Men

Begin *Golden Axe* with 30 Lives and show Death Bringer just who's the boss. Choose a one-player game in the Arcade mode. Next, press and hold Left and Down on your control pad until the warriors spin around continuously. While the warriors are continuing to spin, simultaneously press Buttons A and C. Now, release all of the buttons and press Start. You'll have nine Continue credits instead of three.

Level Select

Tired of messing with the peons? Head straight for Death Bringer with this Level Select trick for the Arcade mode of *Golden Axe*. Wait until the Character Selection screen appears and then press the directional button Down and to the Left so that the three warriors spin around. Now, simultaneously press Button B and Start. If you've done the trick correctly, a "1" will appear in the upper-left corner of the screen. Use Up or Down on the directional pad to change the number and select your starting level.

Axe Death Bringer

Use this trick to bury two or three giant axes in Death Bringer's chest at the end of *Golden Axe*. In a one-player battle, save your magic until the end of the fight. Just after you've struck the blow that defeats Death Bringer, use your magic. Two axes will fly into the air and bury themselves in Death Bringer's chest. In a two-player game, you can see three axes. Have one player back Death Bringer into a corner and slash him just fast enough not to knock him down. While the first player holds him in the corner, the other player should lure the Skeletons to the far side of the room. If the second player can lead the Skeletons around, they won't attack him and they can't hurt the first player. Finally, just as Death Bringer dies, quickly use your magic. If your timing is right, three axes will bury themselves in Death Bringer's chest.

✕ Golden Axe II ✕

Stage Select

Hack your way right to the heart of the matter with this stage select for *Golden Axe II.* While the Intro screen rolls, press and hold Buttons A, B, and C, and press Start. Continue to hold Button A, and release Buttons B and C. Now, while still holding Button A, simultaneously press Buttons B and C again to enter the Options screen.

Continue to hold Button A, but release Buttons B and C once again. Select "Exit" on the Options screen, and while still pressing Button A, simultaneously press Buttons B and C to return to the Main menu.

Continue to hold Button A, and release Buttons B and C. Now, while still holding Button A, simultaneously press Buttons B and C to choose the number of players. Continue to hold all three buttons and press Start to choose the normal game. While still holding all three buttons, highlight your character, press Up, and press Start. Now choose any level in the game.

Bonus Credits

To increase your credits in this fighting fantasy, go to the Options screen. Simultaneously press Buttons A, B, and C, and keep holding them while you enter the Options screen. Release

Button A, but continue to press Buttons B and C. Select Exit and press Start.

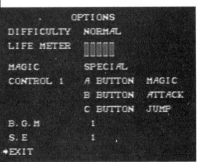

Begin a one- or two-player game, press Start, and then press Button A. You should now have eight credits instead of three.

Unlimited Magic

Make endless magic in *Golden Axe II* with this complicated trick.

Proceed to the end boss of any level, with at least one magic box. During your fight with the boss, press Button A to use your magic and continue to HOLD IT DOWN. Finish off the

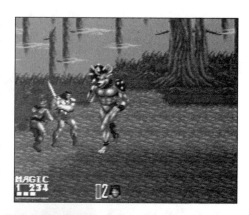

boss (while still holding Button A). Release Button A when the thieves begin to move.

Let them steal two of the magic blocks and don't grab any yourself. When your character reappears in the next level he or she will automatically use a magic spell, even though you don't have any magic boxes left. Afterwards, two rows of magic boxes will appear across the bottom of the screen. Use limitless magic, but don't overcharge the magic or the game will freeze.

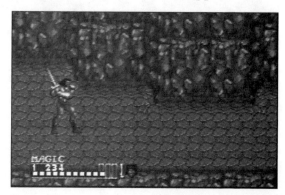

• Green Dog •

Three Flying Discs

Jah mon, you can use this code to snag rapid fire discs. Anytime during play, press Start to pause your game. Then, press Button C, Button A, Button B, Button A, Left, and Left. If you hear a ringing sound, it means the trick worked!

Slow Motion

To play *Green Dog* in slo' mo', begin a regular game and then press Start to pause the game. Then, press Down, Button A, Button C, Up, Left, and Left. You'll hear a ringing sound if you performed the trick correctly. When you're tired of slow

motion, press Start to pause the game again, and then press Left, Right, Up, Down, Button A, and Button C.

Quick Reset

Tired of the beach scene? Reset *Green Dog* the quick way. Just simultaneously press Buttons A, B, C, and Start.

★ Hardball! ★

Championship Passwords

Fire up the bullpen. Here's a line-up of passwords for *Hardball!* that puts you in the World Series:

> **Boston vs. Texas:** iAAEIGbe
> **Boston vs. Chicago (NL):** AEECBGcC
> **California vs. Baltimore:** kcB3GIDi
> **Chicago (NL) vs. Chicago (AL):** 2AAGGAbf
> **Chicago (AL) vs. Atlanta:** 2c36AhbI
> **Cincinnati vs. New York (AL):** dcA2FHD8
> **Detroit vs. Milwaukee:** acA7HJD2
> **Houston vs. Boston:** ccA7EGD6
> **Kansas City vs. Cleveland:** 0cA7IKDa
> **Minnesota vs. Cleveland:** 1cB5IKDa
> **Montreal vs. San Diego:** gAAEGEbk
> **New York (AL) vs. New York (NL):** FAIeBHbf
> **New York (NL) vs. Atlanta:** hAAEHFbh
> **Oakland vs. New York (AL):** jcA2FHD2
> **Philadelphia vs. Los Angeles:** eAAEECb5
> **Pittsburgh vs. San Francisco:** fAAEFDb2
> **San Diego vs. Cleveland:** gcA7HKDg
> **San Francisco vs. Boston:** fcA7EGD3
> **San Francisco vs. Texas:** fcIBGiBA
> **Seattle vs. Toronto:** 3cC6JbDE
> **Texas vs. Detroit:** icB6JaDb

✖ Hard Drivin' ✖

Practice Traffic

Here's a wild code that puts traffic on the practice track in *Hard Drivin'*! First, play a regular game. When you've completed your game and returned to the Title screen, press Button C to go to the Options screen and choose the Practice option.

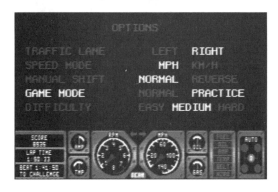

Now, hit Button B and then Button C. Press Start to begin your game. Push the pedal to the metal and practice with all the traffic you'd have in a normal game.

Beat the Phantom Photom

Can't beat the Phantom Photom on *Hard Drivin*'s stunt track? Why not challenge him on the speed track. In the championship lap of the stunt track, all you have to do is turn left instead of going straight ahead. You'll blast over the turn signs and head straight into battle with the Phantom Photom on the speed track.

Moooooo!

There's a cow you can hit just at the beginning of the Stunt Track in *Hard Drivin'*. You'll see her standing next to the barn. All you have to do is aim for her! When you hit her she'll moo!

✳ Heavy Nova ✳

Check Out the Endings

Begin at the end with this *Heavy Nova* trick that enables you to see the game's ending before you've even played the game. Select the game's Configuration screen.

Next, choose "Ultimate" for your Rank, "2 RD 5 Boss" for your Stage, "15" for your Music, and "25" for Sound. Finally, simultaneously press and hold Buttons A, B, and C and then press Start. Psst . . . the only way to check out *Heavy*

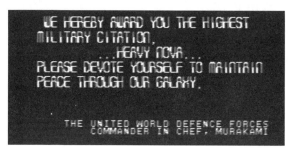

Nova's real ending is to play the game all the way through on the Ultimate setting!

⬧ Hellfire ⬧

Expert Difficulty Mode

Go to *Hellfire* with this trick that warps you to an extra-hard Difficulty mode. Enter the game's Option screen and select "Hard" as your Difficulty mode. Sit and wait for a few minutes. The words on-screen will change to "Yea, right."

When your game begins you're in the Expert mode, and you've also got 99 Continues!

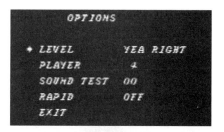

⚖ Herzog Zwei ⚖

Passwords!

Use these passwords to begin with different numbers of wins in *Herzog Zwei*:

> **5 wins:** GGGKHAGOKLO
> **12 wins:** BPHOHACAGML
> **19 wins:** NPLOFOCAGKP
> **22 wins:** IMLPFEGEMLC
> **25 wins:** JAJJBPDNCMC
> **28 wins:** LILOPBDPIKJ
> **31 wins:** JLJOMGJAOKL

Last Level Password

Begin in Round 32 of *Herzog Zwei*:

JLJOIGLAOK

Victory Code for the Blue Army

Lead the Blue Army to victory with this *Herzog Zwei* password:

IEJOJEIKNLA

❄ Hit the Ice ❄

Password

Take a slap shot at the championships with these passwords. You take to the ice as the Sky Blues:

> **Vs. the Blues:** 1QQ3
> **Vs. the Pinks:** 2A13
> **Vs. the Yellows:** 2R93
> **Vs. the Purples:** 3AH3
> **Vs. the Greens:** 3RQ3
> **Vs. the Grays in the Championships:** 4B13

⫙ Humans ⫙

Password

You'll evolve more quickly with these *Humans* passwords for every stage:

Stage 2: VHQBSBGTSFXY	**Stage 6:** DTMFCPWVWFPW
Stage 3: DGTVQBWXBJNC	**Stage 7:** FKNMZXDGJKBW
Stage 4: PBGPGHQZMZGT	**Stage 8:** XSJKNQLMFHWZ
Stage 5: TMHCPYPCPQHQ	**Stage 9:** DVDQTNKTMHSF

Stage 10: VYJMDMPVXHHD	**Stage 45:** TNLQVNQPJBZQ
Stage 11: SDKJRGJHDWZQ	**Stage 46:** PXFCTHKXBVXM
Stage 12: HCDFWZSNXCPH	**Stage 47:** DFGFGFWRRCXW
Stage 13: CBJHXXDMHSVL	**Stage 48:** VNWLGXTRNQCF
Stage 14: FPYBCXGPMPMP	**Stage 49:** ZWNSXGFYNMHS
Stage 15: SRQHNLDRDWPG	**Stage 50:** PDJTKPCTYXDK
Stage 16: NYXKBLPGZXMF	**Stage 51:** HHJYFSXNNPFG
Stage 17: ZGXMLRRNWHLK	**Stage 52:** BPHGLQXJHWJY
Stage 18: RKLLKDZHXNQP	**Stage 53:** BWLPKPNGVFQD
Stage 19: VCRMFKNSRDMF	**Stage 54:** WHYNDZMTYNQT
Stage 20: WDFGNXGRRMPN	**Stage 55:** QDDGVHPGFWLS
Stage 21: YXLPSLBXWHBQ	**Stage 56:** NGJFTTCRVQXKZ
Stage 22: XQHHWPQBJMPC	**Stage 57:** KNCFXXKRMHGV
Stage 23: VYNSJGFQJHCB	**Stage 58:** TSDRLSHXZMJD
Stage 24: SDMFCJKBCJGZ	**Stage 59:** WZWZWZSHCJMH
Stage 25: TKJXCLWLZTWP	**Stage 60:** YNTBXYJYNWLK
Stage 26: CVYXWHYRGDWD	**Stage 61:** FQXKPTYLQJZM
Stage 27: ZFPKPYXJCRGX	**Stage 62:** TZYNMBQRSFZW
Stage 28: QXJKDYRMLSTC	**Stage 63:** BSHJMJTMFCFS
Stage 29: VSPQXYVCLVCB	**Stage 64:** LTLJQVMRYZLM
Stage 30: MFKTJGNSXQJM	**Stage 65:** NCHQVFQXFQZH
Stage 31: FHWHHMTCJSPN	**Stage 66:** MFGLYVGRQVZP
Stage 32: FTWFSBZLYNXS	**Stage 67:** QTSDFMBYTMJJ
Stage 33: LWLSTSLVWDRX	**Stage 68:** CLYBHVQNGBYN
Stage 34: WXTXBCHBWLDG	**Stage 69:** ZWXGZQRGLPPN
Stage 35: ZSRGHXCZYFLQ	**Stage 70:** NCHMNXGHZGLS
Stage 36: ZGHWLXJSXSZM	**Stage 72:** TWJZBHKTMHCP
Stage 37: RSBMVGVSTSBL	**Stage 73:** TQVCXVNFFZZN
Stage 38: CZQNJYZWLWFQ	**Stage 74:** QLMVQJNJMZLQ
Stage 39: ZFPKPYXJCRGX	**Stage 75:** VKPKLSLLYTFC
Stage 40: NSFLKXCBJDWF	**Stage 76:** DWJPYHKDGPYT
Stage 41: HQVQNQVMVGPQ	**Stage 77:** RKLDKFSJBSJZ
Stage 42: FCTRRYFMZMVK	**Stage 78:** TYZNGBCBWPJV
Stage 43: BYNNYHYTGDTC	**Stage 79:** BCDDSNZQZYPC
Stage 44: BDBBGXDYLKHG	**Stage 80:** XPMNWJKFNQZC

✗ The Immortal ✗

Passwords

How many ways are there to die in *The Immortal?* Find out with these lethal passwords:

> **Level 2:** AA9E510006F70
> **Level 3:** F47EF21000E10
> **Level 4:** B5FFF31001EB0
> **Level 5:** B57F943000EB0
> **Level 6:** C65FF53010B41
> **Level 7:** C250F63010AC1
> **Level 8:** E011F730178C1

☷ Indiana Jones and the Last Crusade ☷

Level Select

Crack Indy's whip in any level. Wait until the Lucasfilm logo appears on-screen, and then press Button A, Button B, Button C, Button B, Button C, Button A, Button C, Button A, and Button B. If you've done the trick correctly, the screen turns blue and the word "SHHHHHHH" appears. Now, choose any level you like!

▲ Insector X ▲

Unlimited Continues

Get a buzz on with this easy trick that enables you to add Continues to *Insector X*. When the "Game Over" screen appears, wait for the Continue sign to appear. Press and hold Up and Left on your control pad and press Button C. Each time you press  Button C you add one Continue. You can add up to eight Continues! Repeat this trick whenever you're running low, and keep playing as long as you like.

James "Buster" Douglas ✸ Knockout Boxing ✸

Sound Test

Buster Douglas may be boxing history, but you can still check out the sounds of *James "Buster" Douglas Knockout Boxing*. To activate the trick, press Start on Controller 1 and then select a one- or two-player game. Next, simultaneously press Button C and Start on Controller 2.

```
SOUND TEST

0 EXIT
1 TITLE DEMO
2 CHAMPION
3 VICTORY
4 LAST
5 SELECT
6 DEFEAT
7 OPENING
S SOUND EFFECT
```

⟨ James Pond ⟩

Open the Exit

Sure it sounds fishy but *James Pond* can use this trick to open the Exit before he finishes any level.

When the Title screen appears, simultaneously press Button C and Left on the directional pad, and then press Start. When you wish to actually open the

Exit on a level, simultaneously press Buttons A, B, and C and rotate the directional pad. The Exit opens, and you're free to head for the next mission.

Warp Zones

You'll get hooked on these four warp zones in *James Pond*. Just remember that you can't warp until you've snagged all of the items in each level.

Mission 1: To enter either of the warp zones in Mission 1, first free all of the Lobsters. Once the Lobsters are free you can warp to Mission 6 or Mission 11. To warp to Mission 6, move to the far left between the wall

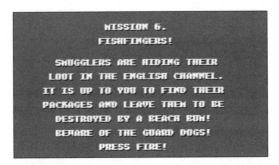

and the home pipe, and then push Down in the middle of the ground.

To warp to Mission 11, swim to the far left and go to the little ledge just out of the water. Stand on top of the ledge and push Down to warp to Mission 11.

Mission 2: When you've got all of the items in Mission 2 you can warp to Mission 5. Simply return to the tube that leads to your house, swim to the left side of the tube in the middle of the ground, and push Down.

Mission 4: To warp to Mission 8, go to the dark water area surrounding the Ship. Search for the long ledge on the left, go to the middle of the ledge, and push Down.

James Pond II: Codename Robocod

Invincibility

He's not scum, but James Pond has a slick trick that'll earn him approximately 10 minutes of Invincibility in *Codename Robocod*. At the

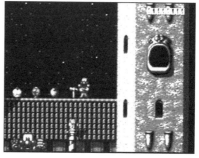

beginning of the game, leap to the roof of the toy factory and grab the items in this order: Cake, Hammer, Earth, Apple, and Tap. This spells CHEAT!

Infinite Lives

Who said fish aren't smart? Earning infinite Lives in *Codename Robocod* is a snapper for James Pond. Enter the first door of the castle and move right until you pass the second set of spikes. Pick up the items inside in this order: Lips, Ice Cream, Violin, Earth,

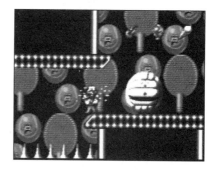

and Snowman. You've spelled LIVES! Hint: Try using this trick in combination with the previous trick and you'll be able to go anywhere you like in the game!

Secret Level

James Pond doesn't "vant to be alone," but he does want to find the entrance to a secret level hidden in Level 1 of *James Pond II: Codename Robocod.* To find it, move as far right as possible and then climb the building. When you reach the far right roof, walk left through the wall. You'll warp to a strange area inside of the factory.

• Jennifer Capriati Tennis •

Grand Slam Password

Not getting enough competition in *Jennifer Capriati Tennis*? Plug in this super password: GRAND.SLAM. Be sure to fill up the

empty spaces in the password with periods. This gives you access to a new lineup of 24 players—12 men and 12 women.

☆ Joe Montana II Sports Talk Football ☆

Password Creation

Bowl everyone over by making your own *Joe Montana II Sports Talk Football* super passwords with this easy trick. Play the game and get any password. Write down the first three letters and the last two letters of

your password. Next, choose one of the following three codes and place it in the middle of your password:

> **First Round:** RSS5B
> **League Championship:** S555D
> **Sega Bowl:** T555H

Team Selection

You can also play as the team of your choice in the First Round Playoffs, Second Round Playoffs, or the Sega Bowl. Just plug the letter that corresponds to your favorite team into one of the following passwords:

First Round Playoffs: _ RSRPO4VKA

Second Round Playoffs: _ RSSPO4XKA

Sega Bowl: _ RSTPO4XKA

A - Atlanta	**K** - Kansas City	**U** - Philadelphia
B - Buffalo	**L** - Houston	**V** - Phoenix
C - Chicago	**M** - Los Angeles (AM)	**W** - Pittsburgh
D - Cincinnati	**N** - Los Angeles (NA)	**X** - San Diego
E - Cleveland	**O** - Miami	**Y** - Seattle
F - Dallas	**P** - Minnesota	**Z** - San Francisco
G - Denver	**Q** - New Orleans	**0** - Tampa Bay
H - Detroit	**R** - New England	**1** - Washington
I - Green Bay	**S** - New York (NA)	
J - Indianapolis	**T** - New York (AM)	

Passwords!

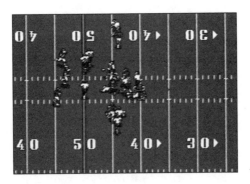

No brains required with these cool passwords that'll enable you to check out different games in *Joe Montana II Sports Talk Football* and leave the passing to us:

San Francisco (Championship): ZABS555DII
San Francisco (Sega Bowl): ZABT555HII
Los Angeles (AM) (Championship): MABS555DIA
Los Angeles (AM) (Sega Bowl): MABT555HIA
Philadelphia (Championship): UX3S555DIA
Philadelphia (Sega Bowl): UX3T555HIA
Los Angeles (NA) (Championship): NAAS555DKA
Los Angeles (NA) (Sega Bowl): NAAT555HKA
Detroit (Championship): HPOS555DIE
Detroit (Sega Bowl): HPOT555HIE
Washington (Championship): 120S555DIA
Washington (Sega Bowl): 120T555HIA

☆ Joe Montana's Sports Talk Football '93 ☆

Code Breakdown

Use this trick to kick off as any *Joe Montana* team you like. Enter the following code, filling in the blank with the letter or number that corresponds to the team you'd like to play as. Fill in the second blank with the number or letter that corresponds to the week you want to play, the Playoffs, or even the Super Bowl:

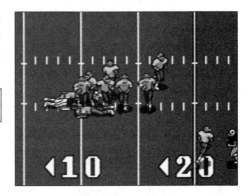

> _YP_???KDJ

Team

B - Falcons	**N** - Chiefs	**Z** - Eagles
C - Bills	**P** - Oilers	**0** - Cardinals
D - Bears	**Q** - Raiders	**1** - Steelers
F - Bengals	**R** - Rams	**2** - Chargers
G - Browns	**S** - Dolphins	**3** - Seahawks
H - Cowboys	**T** - Vikings	**4** - 49ers
J - Broncos	**V** - Saints	**5** - Buccaneers
K - Lions	**W** - Patriots	**6** - Redskins
L - Packers	**X** - Giants	
M - Colts	**Y** - Jets	

Week

D - Week 2	**P** - Week 11
F - Week 3	**Q** - Week 12
G - Week 4	**R** - Week 13
H - Week 5	**S** - Week 14
J - Week 6	**T** - Week 15
K - Week 7	**V** - Week 16
L - Week 8	**W** - 1st Round Play-Offs
M - Week 9	**X** - 2nd Round Play-Offs
N - Week 10	**Y** - Super Bowl

Passwords!

Use these codes to play as the Oilers all the way to the Super Bowl:

Week 1: PGJDCBBBDD	**Week 10:** PGJP??BBDD
Week 2: PGJFFBBBDD	**Week 11:** PGJQ??CBDD
Week 3: PGJGKBBBDD	**Week 12:** PGJR??FBDD
Week 4: PGJHTBBBDD	**Week 13:** PGJS??KBDD
Week 5: PGJJ?BBBDD	**Week 14:** PGJT??YBDD
Week 6: PGJK?CBBDD	**Week 15:** PGJV???BDD
Week 7: PGJL?FBBDD	**Week 16:** PGJW???CDD
Week 8: PGJN?KBBDD	**Week 17:** PGJX???FDD
Week 9: PGJN?TBBDD	**Week 18:** PGJY???KDD

More Passwords!

Or play as the LA Raiders and take them all the way to the Super Bowl:

Week 2: Q4HDCBBBBD	**Week 13:** Q4HRO?FBBD
Week 3: Q4HFFBBBBD	**Week 14:** Q4HSO?HBBD
Week 4: Q4HGKBBBDD	**Week 15:** Q4HTO?RBBD
Week 5: Q4HHTBBBDD	**Week 16:** Q4HVO?8BBD
Week 6: Q4HJOTBBBN	**Playoffs, Week 1:**
Week 7: Q4HKOTBBDN	Q4HWO?8CDD
Week 8: Q4HLOTBBBN	**Playoffs, Week 2:**
Week 9: Q4HMOTBBBN	Q4HXO?8FBD
Week 10: Q4HNOTBBDD	**Super Bowl:**
Week 11: Q4HPO?BBDD	Q4HYO?8KBD
Week 12: Q4HQO?CBBD	

And More Passwords!

Or kick off as the 49ers and play all the way to the Super Bowl:

Week 2: 4W1DCBBBDD	**Week 13:** 4W1R??FBDD
Week 3: 4W1FFBBBDD	**Week 14:** 4W1S??KBDD
Week 4: 4W1GKBBBDD	**Week 15:** 4W1T??TBDD
Week 5: 4W1HTBBBDD	**Week 16:** 4W!V???BDD
Week 6: 4W1J?BBBDD	**Playoffs, Week 1:**
Week 7: 4W1K?CBBDD	4W1W???CDD
Week 8: 4W1L?FBBDD	**NFC Championship:**
Week 9: 4W1M?KBBDD	4W1X???FDD
Week 10: 4W1N?TBBDD	**Super Bowl:**
Week 11: 4W1P??BBDD	4W1Y???KDD
Week 12: 4W1Q??CBDD	

And Even More Passwords!

Kick off in the Super Bowl as the *Sports Talk* team of your choice with this complete set of codes:

Falcons: BK9YZ99?DB	**Vikings:** TK9YZ99?DB
Bills: CK9YZ99?DB	**Cowboys:** HK9YZ99?DB
Bears: DK9YZ99?DB	**Saints:** VK9YZ99?DB
Bengals: FK9YZ99?DB	**Patriots:** WK9YZ99?DB
Browns: GK9YZ99?DB	**Giants:** XK9YZ99?DB
Broncos: JK96Z99?DB	**Jets:** YK9YZ99?DB
Lions: KK9YZ99?DB	**Eagles:** ZK9YZ99?DB
Packers: LK9YZ99?DB	**Cardinals:** OK9YZ99?DB
Colts: MK9YZ99?DB	**Steelers:** 1K9YZ99?DB
Chiefs: NK9YZ99?DB	**Chargers:** 2K9YZ99?DB
Oilers: PK9YZ99?DB	**Seahawks:** 3K9YZ99?DB
Raiders: QK9YZ99?DB	**49ers:** 4K9YZ99?DB
Rams: RK96Z99?DB	**Buccaneers:** 5K9YZ99?DB
Dolphins: SK9YZ99?DB	**Redskins:** 6K9YZ99?DB

☆ John Madden Football ☆

Championship Passwords

Get ready to score with these passwords. You can play as your favorite team in the Championship!

Los Angeles at Miami: 0473176
San Francisco at Denver: 0751000
Minnesota at Denver: 0731000
San Francisco at New England: 0431000
Chicago at New England: 0613000
Philadelphia at Cincinnati: 5555500
Los Angeles at Kansas City: 2452300
Atlanta at Miami: 3452300
New York at Houston: 4452300
Washington at Buffalo: 5450000
Philadelphia at New England: 6450000
Los Angeles at Denver: 7450000
Philadelphia at Denver: 7770000
San Francisco at Houston: 6770000
Atlanta at Pittsburgh: 4770000
Atlanta at Miami: 7777777
Los Angeles at Cincinnati: 6777777
New York at New England: 5777777
Washington at Kansas City: 4777777
Chicago at Pittsburgh: 3777777
Los Angeles at Pittsburgh: 2777777
Philadelphia at Houston: 1777777
Chicago at Denver: 0415000
San Francisco at Buffalo: 0515000
Minnesota at Buffalo: 0535000

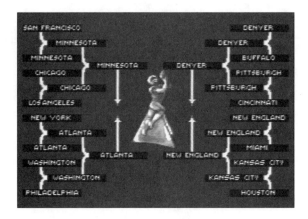

Easy Kickoff Recovery

It's not a boomerang, it's a football. But you can keep possession of it when you're kicking off to the opposing team in *John Madden Football*. First, put the player marker on the kicker. Now, press Button C rapidly as you're about to kick. This makes the kicker leap. If you do the trick just right your kicker will jump on the ball and the screen will say, "Kicking Team Recover!" and the ball is yours!

Stop the Extra Point

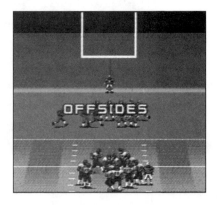

Sure it's unsportsmanlike, but you can stop your opponent from scoring any extra points. Blitz the opposing team off-sides every time your opponent is ready to kick its extra point. When they reach the goal line, let them go for the point. They'll kick it too low every time!

Rev Up the Playoffs

Rewrite history with this trick you can use to add extra options to the Playoff mode in *John Madden Football*. Go to the

Option screen and select Playoff mode. When you see the word "NEW" in the password position press Up on your control pad. The team match-ups will change, with each match-up representing a new playoff schedule. Choose a schedule and then push Down until you reach a

team name. Use Left and Right on the control pad to choose which team in that new playoff schedule you want to play.

✦ John Madden Football '92 ✦

Super Passwords

Just to ensure that you're a permanent couch potato, here are enough passwords to keep you on the field in *John Madden Football '92* for more than a couple of seasons:

CONFERENCE FINALS: SECOND ROUND

Atlanta vs. Washington: C34JKGBM

Buffalo vs. Pittsburgh: B1125TLY

Chicago vs. San Francisco: B1Y97K8J

Cincinnati vs. Oakland: D65ZVTX4

Cleveland vs. Miami: CBW6S0Y4

Dallas vs. N.Y. Giants: BMZ9P687

Denver vs. Seattle: CJWP24GV

Detroit vs. Dallas: B1T5X9YY

Green Bay vs. Dallas: BMXJX4MJ

Houston vs. Seattle: D9YT904R

Houston vs. Buffalo: BY7V7WL4

Houston vs: Buffalo: BKGCB717

Houston vs. Miami: DX056BCV

Indianapolis vs. Oakland: BZC0DR8M

Kansas City vs. Indianapolis: DT5KW087

Kansas City vs. New England: D91K4PGJ

Los Angeles vs. Washington: CFRT5G04

Los Angeles vs. Detroit: BF15XGX4

Miami vs. Buffalo: B426582R

Minnesota vs. San Francisco: BM22KDFM

New England vs. Oakland: D92ZJVCB

New Jersey vs. Buffalo: C1MZKJHR

New Orleans vs. Green Bay: DD2D16WF

New York vs. Washington: BYRNHD1V

Phoenix vs. San Francisco: C39156R1

Pittsburgh vs. Indianapolis: CYVRJWFJ

San Francisco vs. Chicago: C099G4NR

San Francisco vs. Chicago: BCBPTL67

Seattle vs. Houston: BJ962FD1

Tampa Bay vs. New Orleans: CJN6BNBV

Washington vs. New York Giants: B7NJX9PV

CONFERENCE FINALS: THIRD ROUND

Atlanta vs. Philadelphia: C4WNZ3YD
Buffalo vs. Denver: B2S68RYK
Chicago vs. New Orleans: B2PF5N7M
Cincinnati vs. Cleveland: D7X4FBFH
Cleveland vs. Seattle: CCL92PCZ
Dallas vs. Chicago: BNRDN6FY
Denver vs. Cincinnati: CKLWVHBR
Detroit vs. San Francisco: B2J9JPMX
Green Bay vs. San Francisco: BNMNPCN1
Houston vs. Kansas City: FBNY733V
Houston vs. New England: BZZZ5Y05
Houston vs. Denver: BK6GTSVL
Houston vs. Oakland: DYR80FLY
Indianapolis vs. Houston: BZ35MN948
Kansas City vs. Oakland: DVXPBJ2L
Kansas City vs. Denver: FBSPXYH1
Los Angeles vs. New York: CGGX89JC
Los Angeles vs. Philadelphia: CGGZR0JH
Los Angeles vs. Green Bay: BGS9NPZM
Miami vs. Oakland: B5VBZH37
Minnesota vs. New Orleans: BNT55S4L
New England vs. Buffalo: FBT3ZGY3
New Jersey vs. Seattle: C2C39XCM
New Orleans vs. Minnesota: DFTKZD2W
New York vs. Chicago: BZGS8M3B
Oakland vs. New Jersey: C2FGCHF0
Philadelphia vs. Los Angeles: D7CJ866X
Phoenix vs. Oakland: DR85KS35
Phoenix vs. Atlanta: C415842N
Pittsburgh vs. Buffalo: CZKWZH09
San Diego vs. Cleveland: CGV03NJ0
San Francisco vs. Phoenix: C12FRYXZ
San Francisco vs. New York: BC2WWPB8
Seattle vs. Oakland: BK2CG20T
Tampa Bay vs. New York: CKD9GGV2
Washington vs. Chicago: B8DM6Z4N

EASN BOWL

(Note: The NFC team is always the home team)

Atlanta vs. Buffalo: C5LSS65H

Atlanta vs. Houston: D72C835L

Buffalo vs. San Francisco: DWJ4NLPV

Buffalo vs. New York: B3H92V5N

Chicago vs. Kansas City: B3FMKGMT

Chicago vs. Buffalo: B3FM8FB5

Cincinnati vs. San Francisco: C536LLJY

Cincinnati vs. Chicago: D8NG0F5T

Cincinnati vs. Atlanta: D8NDDS0R

Cleveland vs. Washington: CDCHGGS4

Dallas vs. Oakland: BDNZZTR1

Dallas vs. Buffalo: BPGHG9NI

Denver vs. San Francisco: CLB168RX

Detroit vs. Buffalo: BHL50XB6

Detroit vs. New Jersey: B29KH464

Green Bay vs. Cincinnati: BPCYNT78

Green Bay vs. Kansas City: BPCSHGX4

Houston vs. Washington: B0P2Z178

Indianapolis vs. Philadelphia: DKXLZ1LW

Indianapolis vs. Chicago: B0WH6T2K

Kansas City vs. Dallas: DWMS4M9P

Kansas City vs. San Francisco: DWMWRBGS

Kansas City vs. Chicago: FCH2G18B

Kansas City vs. New Orleans: DGXNTKWT

Los Angeles vs. Pittsburgh: BHJFGFVR

Los Angeles vs. Houston: CG68WD8N

Los Angeles vs. Buffalo: CG644SYN

Miami vs. Green Bay: C2Z4ZSZS

Miami vs. New York: B6KFSMCB
Miami vs. Chicago: B6KJB9JD
Minnesota vs. Cleveland: CC50N7W4
Minnesota vs. Seattle: BPKJRXWX
New England vs. New Orleans: DG10WJCT
New England vs. Minnesota: FCKCYYJB
New Jersey vs. Washington: CS41LX68
New Jersey vs. Green Bay: C239PNST
New Orleans vs. Oakland: DGJVYWM3
New York vs. Miami: BTCHRSRX
New York vs. New England: BZ6173NK
Oakland vs. San Francisco: BH4MBJ03
Oakland vs. New York: C25RBY07
Philadelphia vs. Miami: BTGBF4Y9
Philadelphia vs. Buffalo: D73M3BF0
Philadelphia vs. Green Bay: DGMDPPPJ
Phoenix vs. Denver: C5TCNYGV
Pittsburgh vs. Detroit: CZ97JMSL
Pittsburgh vs. Chicago: DWN8M06J
San Diego vs. Washington: C8X8RT1V
San Diego vs. Atlanta: CHK82337
San Francisco vs. Buffalo: C2TL4P94
San Francisco vs. Miami: BDT18GSF
San Francisco vs. Kansas City: CC7CDVLS
Seattle vs. Minnesota: BLTF857X
Seattle vs. New Orleans: D5KT9LWW
Tampa Bay vs. Buffalo: CK5GV777
Tampa Bay vs. Cincinnati: DNBS1KMB
Washington vs. Cincinnati: FB16WJWP
Washington vs. Buffalo: B84R03CS

● Jordan vs. Bird: Super One-on-One ●

Extra Time

This trick snares you a ton of extra time in the One-on-One mode of *Jordan vs. Bird.* When you're playing in the One-on-One mode, try to press Start to pause the game just as the timer hits 00.00 at the end of the fourth period. Then call a Time Out. If you manage to time this correctly, you'll discover that instead of being over, your game continues for 36 more minutes! If you repeat this trick when the time runs out the second time, you'll continue with 100 more minutes! Whew! Remember that you can't press Start when you're holding the basketball, so strategize accordingly. If it doesn't work, don't be afraid to try again. The timing on this trick is almost impossible.

☆ Jurassic Park ☆

Passwords

To help you cover your Jurassic, here are passwords for both Dr. Grant and the Raptor for every level of the game on all the difficulty settings! All of the Dr. Grant passwords give you 60 units of ammo for every weapon.

Dr. Grant

Easy
Level 1: 0VVVVVTO
Level 2: 2VVVVVTQ
Level 3: 4VVVVVTQ
Level 4: 6VVVVVTS
Level 5: 8VVVVVTU
Level 6: AVVVVVT2
Level 7: CVVVVVT4

Normal
Level 1: 0VVVVVUP
Level 2: 2VVVVVUR
Level 3: 4VVVVVUT
Level 4: 6VVVVVUV
Level 5: 8VVVVVU1
Level 6: AVVVVVU3
Level 7: CVVVVVU5

Hard
Level 1: 0VVVVVVQ
Level 2: 2VVVVVVS
Level 3: 4VVVVVVU
Level 4: 6VVVVVV0
Level 5: 8VVVVVV2
Level 6: AVVVVVV4
Level 7: CVVVVVV6

Raptor

Easy
Level 1: G21G0014
Level 2: I21G0016
Level 3: K21G0018
Level 4: M21G001A
Level 5: 021G001C

Normal
Level 1: G21G0025
Level 2: I21G0027
Level 3: K21G0029
Level 4: M21G002B
Level 5: 021G002D

Hard
Level 1: G21G0036
Level 2: I21G0038
Level 3: K21G003A
Level 4: M21G003C
Level 5: 021G003E

See the Game's Credits

See *Jurassic Park*'s credits the easy way with this simple password: FREIHEIT

♨ Kid Chameleon ♨

Skip Straight to the Final Boss

Don't kid around. Head straight to the final battle in *Kid Chameleon*. Advance to Blue Lake Woods II and work your way to the very end of the level — but don't touch the flag. Jump to the very last prize block and simultaneously push the Jump and Special buttons and Down and Right on your control pad. You'll warp straight to the final boss.

5,000 Bonus Points

It's amazingly easy to earn a special Bonus of 5,000 points on any level in *Kid Chameleon*. All you have to do is go through the entire level without grabbing any special items. If you make it you'll be awarded a special "No Prize Bonus" of 5,000 points.

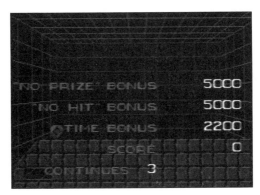

♦ Krusty's Super Fun House ♦

Passwords

Ha, ha, ha! Here are passwords for every level in the Fun House:

Level 2: WHOAMAMA
Level 3: FLANDERS
Level 4: BROCKMAN
Level 5: SIDESSHOW

Super Password

Give Krusty infinite Lives and an open door to any level he likes. Plug in the password SMAILLIW and begin your game.

• Lakers vs. Celtics and the NBA Playoffs •

Championship Passwords

If hoops are your thing, slam dunk these champion- ship passwords for *Lakers vs. Celtics:*

Boston Celtics vs. San Antonio Spurs: CZ2 QKT

Chicago Bulls vs. Portland Trailblazers: 6RQ QJJ

Chicago Bulls vs. Los Angeles Lakers: PJM RJT

Detroit Pistons vs. Los Angeles Lakers: G72 QOJ

Detroit Pistons vs. San Antoinio Spurs: H76 QJK

Los Angeles Lakers vs. Chicago Bulls: LLQ RJK

Philadelphia 76ers vs. San Antonio Spurs: H12 QJT

Phoenix Suns vs. Boston Celtics: RP2 HJT

Phoenix Suns vs. Chicago Bulls: 6P2 GJS

Portland Blazers vs. Boston Celtics: TY6 HJK

San Antonio Spurs vs. Philadelphia 76ers: 8W2 QJS

✦ The Last Battle ✦

Continue

If it's the last thing you do, continue your game with this endless Continue trick for *Last Battle*. When your game ends, simultaneously press Buttons A, B, and C. Continue to press and hold these three

buttons, and hit Start four times. If you've finished Chapter One you'll be able to choose to select any Chapter to begin play on, up to the Chapter you reached. Psst . . . this trick only works when you've finished Chapter One.

✈ LHX Attack Chopper ✈

Passwords

Take to the skies with these *LHX* passwords:

Libya
Majestic Twelve:
   CQAAAFA
Anterior Nova:
   CQAAIEA
Reindeer Flotilla:
   CQAAQHA
Phoenix: CQAAYGA
Rainbow Veil: CQAAAVC
Chess: CQAAIUC

Lobster Quadrille:
   CQAAQXC
Hen House: CQAAYWC
Desert Two: CQAABFE
Flaming Arrow: CQAAJEE
Plain Aria: CQIERDG

Central Europe
Domino Mirror: CSIEIYE
Chess: CSIEQ6E
Arc Lite: CSIEY4E
Anterior Nova: CSIEBJC
Reindeer Flotilla: CSIEJIC
Hop Toad: CSIERLC
Olympic Torch: CSIEZKC
Lobster Quadrille: CSIEBZA
Grand Theft Hokum: CSIEJYA
Flaming Arrow: CSIER6A

Vietnam
Lobster Quadrille: CQIEZCG
Reindeer Flotilla: CQIEBRE
Flaming Arrow: CQIEJQE
Hen House: CQIERTE
Lava Lamp: CSIEZSA
Anterior Nova: CSIEAJG
Gemini: CSIEIIG
Chess: CSIEQL6
Binary Rainstorm: CSIEYKG
Freedom Train: CSIEAZE

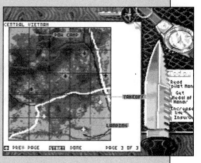

❊ Lightening Force ❊

99 Ships

 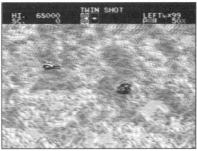

Soar through *Lightening Force* the easy way, by using this trick to begin with 99 Lives. Wait until the words "Press Start" appear on the Title screen and then simultaneously press Buttons A and Start. When the Configuration screen appears, highlight "Stock Ship" and set the number to zero. Now, begin your game. You'll discover that you've got 99 ships.

✂ Lotus Turbo Challenge ✂

Passwords

Racers start your engines. Here are some revved up passwords for *Lotus Turbo Challenge*:

Track 2:	Sleepers
Track 3:	Herbert
Track 4:	Business
Track 5:	ApplePie
Track 6:	Standish
Track 7:	Mallow
Track 8:	Tea Cup

Super Passwords

Shhhhhhh . . . it's a secret. Plug in these two passwords to access special *Lotus Turbo Challenge* options. To race through the entire circuit without worrying about qualifying, plug in

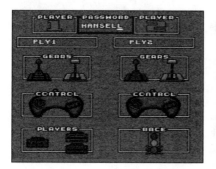 

the password MANSELL. No matter how poorly you race, you'll automatically qualify for the next round.

To race with a super-powered Lotus, plug in the password SLUGPACE. Now you're behind the wheel of a racer that can go from zero to 60 m.p.h. in seconds.

🚜 M-1 Abrams Battle Tank 🚜

Invincibility

You'll be saying "Tanks for the memories" with this invincibility trick for *M-1 Abrams Battle Tank*. During the demo screen press Button B two times, Button C, Button B, Button C three times, Button B, Button C, Button B two times, and Button C.

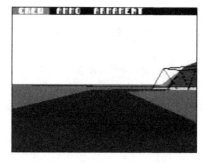

❄ Mario Lemieux Hockey ❄

Final Password!

Skate straight to the final round of play with this *Mario Lemieux* password:

> E7BE MBD2 EJFC

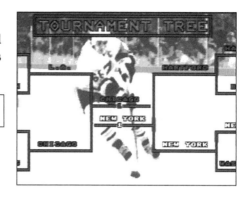

Take New York to the Championship

Use these passwords to take New York to the championship in *Mario Lemieux Hockey*:

Quarter-Finals:
New York vs. Pittsburgh—
QX3N TFE3 CLC3

Semi-Finals: New York vs. Boston—QP3N TFG3 CLC3

Finals: New York vs. Los Angeles—Q75N VFG3 CLD3

⊕ Marvel Land ⊕

Stage Select

Have a marvelous time in *Marvel Land* with this cool password that enables you to choose any level: ARDE. Just enter the

password and a Round Select screen will appear that you can use to access all of the game's stages.

Passwords

You can use the password trick on the previous page to choose any stage in *Marvel Land*, or you can simply enter one of the following codes:

Round 1-2: XIGN	**Round 3-1:** AOWM
Round 1-3: NSOG	**Round 3-2:** GVKJ
Round 1-4: QOCT	**Round 3-3:** RBJW
Round 1-5: USOG	**Round 3-4:** XYNK
Round 1-6: XULW	**Round 3-5:** BTIS
Round 1-7: WIXT	**Round 3-6:** STER
Round 2-1: PAYX	**Round 3-7:** HCHI
Round 2-2: ZISY	**Round 4-1:** SMOK
Round 2-3: AUXY	**Round 4-2:** RUAO
Round 2-4: XTLG	**Round 4-3:** QRUP
Round 2-5: ALWN	**Round 4-4:** AUNT
Round 2-6: ZTOX	**Round 4-5:** WTTH
Round 2-7: ZWMO	**Round 4-6:** ARDE

🌟 Mazin Saga: Mutant Fighter 🌟

Fight the Bosses

Here's a trick that enables you to fight the bosses without fighting through the stages. Go to the game's Option screen, highlight Sound Test, and select Sound 18. Then, choose the Sound Effects Test option and select Sound 72. Exit the mode and press Start. Begin your game, and you'll zap straight to the first stage boss.

🎖 Mercs 🎖

Full Power

 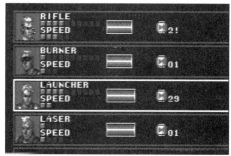

Power up your lifeline with this trick for the Original mode in *Mercs*. When your character touches a red First Aid box and his power begins to fill up, quickly change to each of your other characters in order to restore their energy, too!

✈ Midnight Resistance ✈

Skip Stages

You won't be in the dark anymore with this *Midnight Resistance* trick that enables you to select stages. Wait for the Title screen to appear.

When the word "Start" is highlighted in red, press and hold Button C, and then press Start. When the game begins, press Start again to pause it. Now press Button A and you'll skip to the next stage. Repeat this procedure any time during your game!

♊ Might and Magic ♊

Ultimate Power-Up

Might sometimes does make right, so use this trick to power-up your characters with some strange skills in *Might and Magic*. Choose View Character any time dur-

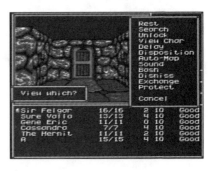

ing your game. When the message "View Which?" appears on-screen, press and hold Left, Button A, and Button C in that order. Release all three buttons simultaneously. You'll see some strange super-powered characters on-screen. Use your control pad to scroll Left through these characters and trade their treasures to your party. You can instantly arm your party with the finest weapons *Might and Magic* has to offer! Try using this code in different situations for different results.

Chow Down!

Make miracles in *Might and Magic* by feeding your entire party without buying any food. To perform this trick, go to your Command screen, choose Share, and then Food. Repeat this procedure several times to increase your entire food supply. You

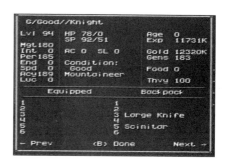

can even end up with more than 40 units.

★ Mike Ditka's Power Football ☆

Play to the Championship as Washington

Kick off in the Mike Ditka Power Bowl Championship as Washington or Miami with these gridiron passwords:

Conference Title: Washington vs. Atlanta - tjF1L4
World Championship: Washington vs. New York - tjF1M0

Conference Title: Miami vs. Cleveland - xjPlDm
World Championship: Miami vs. San Francisco - xjPlEi

⊕ Moonwalker ⊕

Turn into a Robot

Catch a falling star in *Moonwalker* and transform Michael into a robot. In different levels of the game, you can rescue a particular child, grab the shooting star that streaks by, and turn into a super powerful robot.

In Level 2-1, rescue the child in the third window on the right of the roof of Club 30.

In Level 2-2, head to the top of the garage and rescue the only child hidden on that level.

In Level 2-3, use the elevator to go up one floor and then rescue the child hidden on that floor.

In Level 3-2, rescue the child in the second tombstone to the right of where the level begins.

In Level 3-3, head to the left side of the waterfall, look up, and save the child just above you.

Level Select

Dance circles around Mr. Big with this two controller trick that enables you to choose any level in *Moonwalk-*
er, except Level 6, the final level. On Controller 2, simultaneously press and hold Up, Left, and Button A, and then hit Start two times on Controller 2. The words "Round 1" will appear on-screen. Use your directional pad to change the round numbers and then press Start to begin your game.

✳ Mortal Kombat ✳

Play Mode A

The regular game not tough enough for you? To play the original arcade-style Mode A play—complete with the Fatality Moves, —press Button A, Button B, Button A, Button C, Button A, Button B, and Button B.

Killer Kode

Use this top secret code for some mortal fun. When the Game Start/Options screen appears, press Down, Up, Left, Left, Button A, Right, and Down (hey, that's D, U, L, L, A, R, D!).

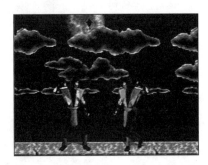

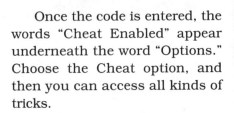

Once the code is entered, the words "Cheat Enabled" appear underneath the word "Options." Choose the Cheat option, and then you can access all kinds of tricks.

Fighter 1 and 2: Lets you choose which of the seven Kombatants you want to use for the various options below.

Plan Base—Random, One, Two, Three, or Four: Access the computer's basic strategies for fighting human opponents.

Chop-Chop: Choose from five different bonus round substances in the "Test Your Might" demo.

1Play and 2Play Chop: Determines how often the player is given a chance to "Test Your Might." X0 is not at all, X1 is after every match, X2 is after every two matches, etc.

Demo: Watch the Cameo, Biographies (ending stories), and Battle Play for the current Fighter 1. Chop-Chop enables you to play the "Test Your Might" bonus round with the currently selected fighters. Choosing Medal will show you the pre-match screen for a two-player game, using the arena and players currently selected. Press Button A, B, or C to begin the demo

FLAG0: This option weakens Player 2. It only takes one attack by Player 1 to defeat Player 2. The exception is Goro. He'll be fine in the first fight, but weakened in the second and third fights.

FLAG1: Cripples Player 1.

FLAG2: Go straight to Reptile! You'll see all of the different silhouettes that go across the moon. Once this option is activated, you've just got to defeat your opponent in the Pit with a Double Flawless and a Finishing Move, and then you fight Reptile.

FLAG3: Choose the Pit as your first map background. The initials BYC and a bouncing face will scroll across the Pit's moon. This option won't work unless you choose the Pit as your first fight.

FLAG4: This option makes the Reptile clue messages appear before every match. It also weakens your opponent in the second and third rounds.

FLAG5: Activate this flag for unlimited continues.

FLAG6: When this flag is on, the computer characters always execute their Finishing Moves.

FLAG7: Turn this on to fight in the Courtyard against unusually tough opponents.

BLOOD: This turns the blood on or off!

CHEAT: This turns the Cheat Mode on or off.

1ST MAP: Use this option to select the forum for your first fight. If you choose the Pit, you'll automatically have the opportunity to fight Reptile.

Muhammad Ali's Heavyweight Boxing

Weird Time at the Rinky Dink

Ready for a weird *Muhammad Ali* match? Enter the code: H070007Z in the Tournament mode. You'll be fighting as Ali with a ranking of one, no wins, and no losses. Your opponent will be a strange gent by the name of Ali Muhammad. This guy looks strangely familiar except for the white eyebrows, moustache, gloves, trunks, and boots. This opponent looks rickety, but he's tough. When you lose, and this strange fighter's mug appears on-screen, he'll be minus his head and a small body of the ref will be in its place.

For a more run-of-the-mill fight, plug in the password H074W57Z in the Tournament mode. You're Ali with a number two ranking, 40 wins, and no losses. You're fighting for the title.

✦ M.U.S.H.A. ✦

Round Select

To choose any round in *M.U.S.H.A.* wait for the Sega logo to appear on-screen. Then, press Reset. Wait for the Sega sign to reappear, and press Reset again. Repeat this procedure eight more times.

Finally, let the Title screen appear on-screen and enter the Options menu while holding Down and Left on your control pad. The words "Round" will now appear underneath "Game Level." Choose Round and use Right and Left on your control pad to select any stage!

Five Bonus Lives

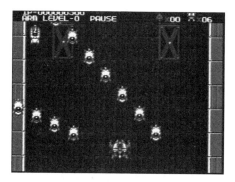

Use this trick to earn five Extra Lives in *M.U.S.H.A.* Wait until your game begins, and then press Start to pause. Next, press Right, Down, Right, Down, Left, Up, Left, Up, Button B, Button C, Button A, and Start.

Begin with 20 Options

Use this trick to begin *M.U.S.H.A.* with 20 options. When your game begins, press Start to pause the game, and then press Up three times, Down three times, Left three times, Right three times, Button C two times, Button B, Button A, and Start on your control pad.

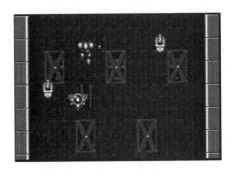

Play with Full Fire Power

Power-up your ship in *M.U.S.H.A.* whenever you like with this slick trick. Any time during play, press Start to pause the game. Next, press Button B two times, Button C, Button B two times, Button C, Up, Down, and Button A.

• Mutant League Football •

Mutant Bowl Passwords

Ugh, grunt, grrr. Use these codes to head straight to the *Mutant League* Bowl as the team of your choice:

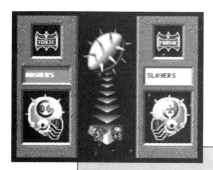

Darkstar Dragons - FMK3XYSL1Q
Deathskin Razors - 1CK111111H
Icebay Bashers - 2CK111111D
Killer Konvicts - HGK111111J
Midway Monsters - 3CK111111F
Misfit Demons - JH111111G
Psycho Slashers - GMK111111D
Rad Rockers - 5CK111111M
Road Warriors - BDK111111J
Screaming Evils - KLK111111L
Sixty Whiners - CBK111111J
Slaycity Slayers - LJK111111M
Terminator Trolz - MLK111111J
Turbo Techies - NMK111111Q
Vile Vulgars - 4CK111111L
War Slammers - DCK1111112

🏒 NHL Hockey 🏒

Final Round Passwords

Make a power play for the Stanley Cup with the following one-player *NHL Hockey* passwords for all 22 teams:

Boston Bruins vs. Calgary Flames:
GBVD2YRDJ1PGXCGZ

Boston Bruins vs. Vancouver Canucks:
H5MNCCBX4L4H73Z7

Buffalo Sabers vs. Detroit Red Wings:
B7M6RKZFGW26RYDY

Buffalo Sabers vs. Los Angeles Kings:
BN6YXDK951C0YVX8

Calgary Flames vs. Pittsburgh Penguins:
HL5S042YKCV0PFVH

Calgary Flames vs. New York Rangers:
H5L19CYS9FPZPT22

Chicago Blackhawks vs. Pittsburgh Penguins:
HZ2NY6ZWD25X7CPY

Detroit Red Wings vs. Montreal Canadiens:
FFB1LC1K10YVW0V2

Detroit Red Wings vs. New York Rangers:
B13XFTJ77WJBKRX9

Edmonton Oilers vs. Pittsburgh Penguins:
D2FV7SNMPJJRX35K

Hartford Whalers vs. Calgary Flames:
FZV795XCZ344SNSM

Hartford Whalers vs. Detroit Red Wings:
BWP0GT1P98NYVXHR

Los Angeles Kings vs. Buffalo Sabers:
G757ZSVP2WF8VW02

Los Angeles Kings vs. Boston Bruins:
HL43CZJNMRXN9Y8D

Minnesota North Stars vs. Pittsburgh Penguins:
HZ2B48N9HY55MK8W

Montreal Canadiens vs. Calgary Flames:
HL61CRJ3NX49PT3K

Montreal Canadiens vs. Los Angeles Kings:
G2SR64PVLTS2NPZR

New Jersey Devils vs. Chicago Blackhawks:
CLNCPPYH63GZVH07

New York Islanders vs. Los Angeles Kings:
CZMW98Y9CW3L29N8

New York Rangers vs. Los Angeles Kings:
G79HYM85VTNCKCSW

New York Rangers vs. Vancouver Canucks:
B17F5MF0ZG238V8F

Philadelphia Flyers vs. Calgary Flames:
HTPTRGHGWB79VHZP

Philadelphia Flyers vs. Detroit Red Wings:
B7P5P9Z91DVMK3VN

Pittsburgh Penguins vs. Calgary Flames:
BN7Y34ZSP46D1T4R

Pittsburgh Penguins vs. Minnesota North Stars:
GPVKNVZZVHW0BBS5

Quebec Nordiques vs. Los Angeles Kings:
C42Z8MN44Y4YLG39

St. Louis Blues vs. Montreal Canadiens:
GBSGTNMD7BR21T7J

St. Louis Blues vs. Pittsbrugh Penguins:
C4Z3S8NMFJG3JMK0

San Jose Sharks vs. Boston Bruins:
G75X97V90T0M6MNY

San Jose Sharks vs. Pittsburgh Penguins:
FLWTN36GNHNT4SZN

Toronto Maple Leafs vs. Boston Bruins:
B1261BH09HHGMZF3

Toronto Maple Leafs vs. Hartford Whalers:
DHYLKFDGB0B402SP

Vancouver Canucks vs. Hartford Whalers:
B14HVDC47BGV4D26

Vancouver Canucks vs. Washington Capitals:
B14J9L0YLTCP9LDS

Washington Capitals vs. Detroit Red Wings:
DBK2LW2XP0JHHW9Y

Winnipeg Jets vs. Buffalo Sabers:
HFNB55PZ9WLTMZSN

Winnipeg Jets vs. Pittsburgh Penguins:
CLKT82F6BXBLZLLX

Teammate Championship Passwords

Grab a buddy and get ready to ice these *NHL Hockey* Stanley Cup Championship passwords:

> **Boston Bruins:** HL6F13TM52R5HW72
>
> **Buffalo Sabers:** B7M9DZHBH1TB9Y9G
>
> **Calgary Flames:** GW7399BL8HLB2J1K
>
> **Detroit Redwings:** DWX6O90L855MK33F
>
> **Edmonton Oilers:** BWNV5267XBO9Y65K
>
> **Minnesota North Stars:** CD2T1XN89S0LZLLY
>
> **Montreal Canadiens:** HFRNGT6RVK6Y29JJ
>
> **New York Islanders:** D70X4KKN5LXJCTTJ
>
> **New York Rangers:** HZ684PMY159BPFXF
>
> **Pittsburgh Penguins:** FZXZPR3PW6CDD9HL
>
> **Quebec Nordiques:** BN7M6H0686FWHHY3
>
> **St. Louis Blues:** H5KVFGM0489GDKFJ
>
> **San Jose Sharks:** BN6FGL4C72VMK3RD
>
> **Toronto Maple Leafs:** B12835LMKGF6CTXW
>
> **Vancouver Canucks:** D7YB87ZY88XYP5YF
>
> **Winnipeg Jets:** CS2YMZ9DJ0BBBBKJ

1991 Playoff Password

This password is easy to remember, and it enables you to hit the ice as the Chicago Blackhawks in a playoff scenario based on the 1991 setup. Just enter all *B*s as your password.

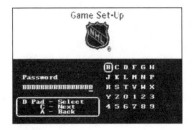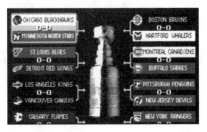

Onslaught

End Password

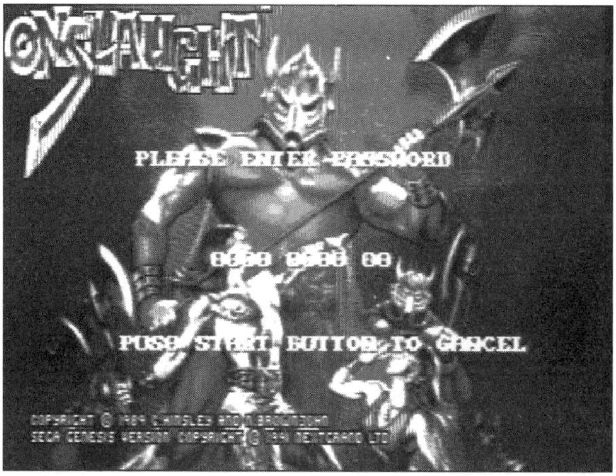

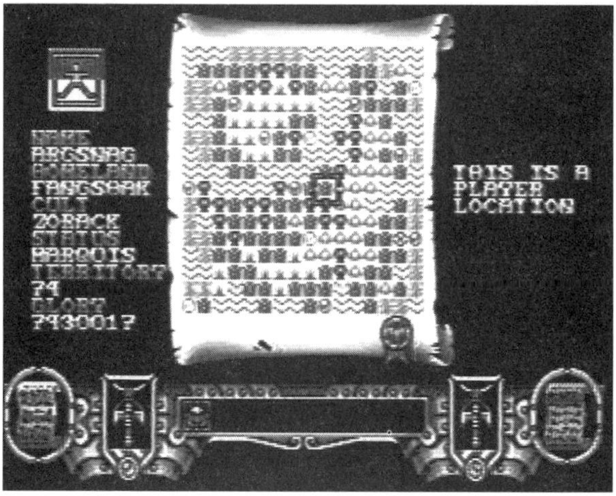

Cut to the chase with this simple *Onslaught* password that enables you to begin with all of the territories conquered except for 10:

0000,0000,00

▤ OutRun ▤

Extra Difficulty

Hey, hot shot! *OutRun* isn't tough enough for you? Here's a trick that gives you an extra difficulty level. All you have to do is press Button C ten times

when the Title screen appears. Now go to the Option screen and you'll discover a new new difficulty level called "Hyper."

New Ending

A little swap on the score board is all it takes to see a different ending sequence in *OutRun*. Just enter your name as ENDING on the score board and go. Your car automatically begins to drive down the road, stopping at different billboards. The names of the game's designers are on the billboards. When the car passes the last billboard, it stops, the couple gets out, and the girl receives the trophy. Stay tuned as she hands it to the guy, gives him a kiss, and the words "Congratulations" appear on-screen.

✮ Phantasy Star II ✮

Invincibility

To become invincible in *Phantasy Star II*, repeatedly press Button C and then B while you hold the directional pad in the direction you wish to move. You'll be able to explore the terrain without fighting any battles.

Slow Motion

Go slow and steady in *Phantasy Star II* with this wild trick. Press Start to pause the game, and then press and hold Button B. For super slow motion, hit Button C repeatedly while the game is paused.

Change the Music

Use this trick if you'd like the music to stay the same when you enter a town or village in *Phantasy Star II*. Activate the Slow Motion trick (see above). Enter a town or village (while still in slow motion) and press Start. The music stays the same! You can use this trick anywhere in the game.

🏛 Phelios 🏛

Extra Continues

Saddle up and begin *Phelios* with nine Continues instead of three. All you have to do is go to the Chapter 1 screen and then press Button C, Button A, Button B, Button A, Button C, Button A, Button B, and Button A.

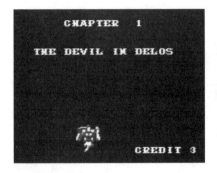

Tons of 1-Ups

Antaeus likes to put gamers on the hot seat, but you can use this trick to battle the Round 4 boss in *Phelios* and score tons of 1-Ups. While you fight Antaeus, move to the far right-hand side of the screen where his fire can't hurt you. Now, fire rapidly

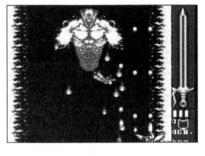

and keep shooting to destroy the hands that fly out of the fire. You'll score lots of points and earn about one 1-Up per minute.

See Artemis

If you're lucky you can score big and make the wall fall down around Artemis in *Phelios*. To make the wall completely fall you must have a score of 200,000 points or higher. Don't look!

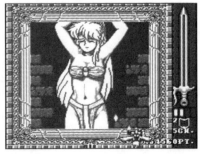

⚖ Pit-Fighter ⚖

Extra Continues

Keep on fighting in *Pit-Fighter* with this slick Continue trick. Play your favorite character until you're almost out of life. Pause your game and plug in Controller 2. Un-pause the game and press Start on Controller 2. Choose your fighter and you'll begin with three extra Continues. Now, beat up your former fighter! Use your new fighter to beat the meat into the streets through the remaining matches of the game!

Grudge Match

Are you ready for a three-way Grudge Match in *Pit Fighter*? To find out, press Button A to enter the game's Option screen. Next, have Player One select his fighter. Player Two should

wait to press Start until the words "Grudge Match" appear on-screen. Now, Player Two should select his fighter and the two will join in a fight to the finish against the computer!

⊕ **Populous** ⊕

Level Select

Go forth and multiply, but first choose any level in *Populous*. Select "New Game." Next, press Button B and then press Up or Down on the control pad until numbers appear on-screen. Choose any stage you like by selecting different numbers. To choose a particular level, put in a number that is five times the number of the level you'd like to play.

Passwords

Think it's easy playing the supreme being? Use these higher level passwords to see just how tough it can get in *Populous*!

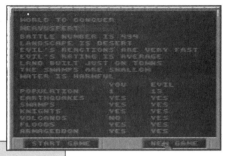

World 100: CALEOLD
World 200: EOAMPMET
World 300: BILQAZOUT
World 400: BADMEILL
World 494: WEAVUSPERT
(This is the last world)

✳ Powerball ✳

Passwords!

Bounce into the championship game and the finals as China with these *Powerball* passwords:

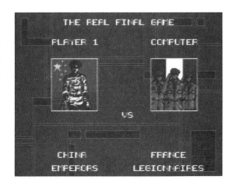

First Championship game vs. Japan: PVDCR
Second Championship game vs. Germany: CMOPE
Semi-Final Game vs. Canada: BFOOE
Final Game vs. France: OADBR

Hidden Teams

Surprise! There are four hidden teams in *Powerball*. Use this trick to select any one of them as your team. During the original team display, press Button B two times, Button C, Button B two times, and Button C. Finally, press Down on the directional pad to reveal the four hidden teams.

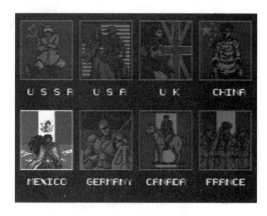

℣ Predator 2 ℣

Passwords

Annihilate the Predators with these easy-to-remember codes:

Stage 2: Killers
Stage 3: Camoflauge
Stage 4: Los Angeles
Stage 5: Subterror
Stage 6: Total Body

★ QuackShot Starring Donald Duck ★

Unlimited Donalds

Now don't quack up. There are several locations in *QuackShot* where you can rack up tons of Extra Lives.

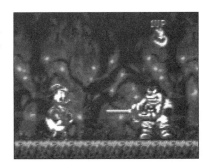

In the middle of the first half of the Transylvania area (outside of the castle) you'll meet up with a member of the Ducky Gang who holds a 1-Up.

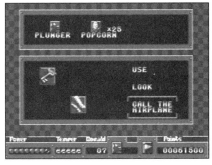

Snag the 1-Up and proceed through the level until you reach the flag.

Instead of entering the castle, call the airplane. Choose Transylvania again on the Map screen and return through the first half of the level — backwards!

The 1-Up and all other special items will have returned. Repeat this procedure until you have a full stockpile of Extra Lives.

More Unlimited Donalds

Here's another spot where you can waddle your way to tons of Donalds in *Quack-Shot*. First, you'll need to get the Bubble Gum Blaster in Duckburg. Next, go to Dracula's Castle in Transylvania. Move forward until you reach the first large stack of barrels. Blast the last barrel on the second row to reveal a 1-Up. Now, exit the castle and then return. You can grab the 1-Up again. Repeat this procedure to earn plenty of 1-Ups.

And Even More Unlimited Donalds

Ahoy there matey! You can also rack up tons of Extra Lives in the Viking Ship area of the game. Climb the mast in the elevator and grab all of the bags of money. When you reach the top of the elevator, head to the right. Follow the rope path down and you'll find a 1-Up. Next, retrace your steps, leave the screen, and repeat this procedure until you have as many Lives as you like.

Bubble Gum Bonus

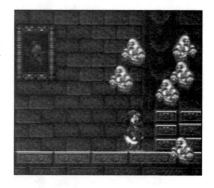

There's a place in *QuackShot* where Donald can get all of the gum he needs and more for his Bubble Gun. Go to Transylvania. When you reach the set of blocks shown in the screen, destroy all of the blocks and then jump on top of the one that remains behind. Each time you jump, new gum will appear. Gather it and jump again. Donald's stoked!

Egyptian Shortcut

Donald's a duck not known for his speed, but there is a way to make a quick exit out of Egypt

in *QuackShot*. When you reach the first ladder in the level, scale it and the wall. When you reach the top waddle right and you're outta there.

Stop the Wall from Falling

There's an easy way to keep the wall from falling on Donald in the Egyptian area of *QuackShot*. When Donald reaches the Falling Wall, simply have him waddle to the right and jump on the icons in the following order: Sun, Moon, Star.

✗ Quad Challenge ✗

Heat Passwords

You'll finish first when you use these codes to skip to different heats in *Quad Challenge*:

Heat 1: EASY
Heat 2: ECGT
Heat 3: M4SR
Heat 4: DTXG
Heat 5: 9F2J
Heat 6: 13RB
Heat 7: PNF5
Heat 8: CR11
Heat 9: 5JE8
Heat 10: 8SWG
Heat 11: HGLY
Heat 12: Q44E
Heat 13: WHCM
Heat 14: TVGZ
Heat 15: SNDN
Heat 16: B16A

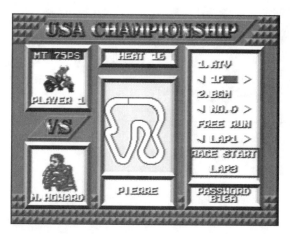

● R.B.I. Baseball 3 ●

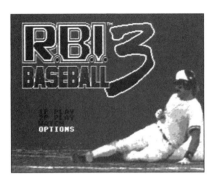

Sound Test

Take yourself out to *R.B.I. 3*s sound test before you step into the batter's box. Wait for

the Title screen to appear and select the Options screen. Next, choose the Continue option and then press Button A two times. The Sound Test will appear on-screen. Use Left and Right on your control pad to select a sound, Button A to begin the sound, and Button B to stop it. Hit Start to return to your game.

Tengen Team Passwords

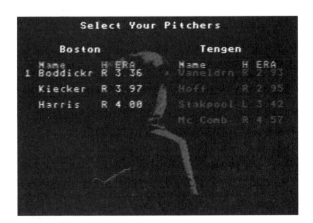

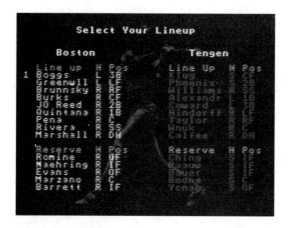

You won't strike out with these passwords for the Tengen Team in *R.B.I. Baseball 3*:

> **Tengen Team vs. Boston:** GFUQ37G2W
> **Tengen Team vs. Toronto:** RJ2Q37G2WP

● R.B.I. Baseball '93 ●

Passwords

Play ball with this *R.B.I.* password trick that enables you to take the plate as any of the '92 teams against the Tengen team. The difficulty is medium. Fill in the blank with the letter or number that corresponds to the team you wish to use. The password is:

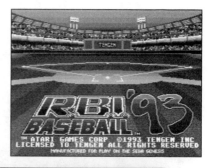

D_WWD2CHCCSY

D_WWD2CHCCSY

A - Los Angeles
B - Florida
C - Missouri
D - Baltimore
E - Coloraco
F - Chicago (NL)
G - New York (AL)
H - Boston
I - Michigan
J - Cincinnati   **W** - California
K - Chicago (AL)   **X** - Texas
L - Allstars (AL)   **Y** - Kansas City
O - Milwaukee   **Z** - Oklahoma
P - St. Louis   **9** - Atlanta
Q - San Diego   **8** - Pittsburgh
R - New York (NL)   **7** - Houston
S - Cleveland   **6** - Toronto
T - Seattle   **4** - Detroit
U - San Francisco   **3** - Philadelphia

♣ Raiden Trad ♣

Restore Your Power-Ups

You'll raid *Raiden Trad* with this quick Power-Up trick. If your ship is fully powered-up, a Fairy will appear when you're blown up. Shoot the Fairy and your lost Power-Up items will reappear. If the Fairy releases a "P," first grab your missile Power-Up, and then grab the "P" to maximize your missile power.

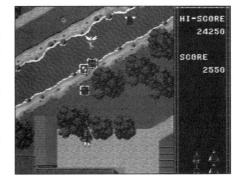

⚔ Rambo III ⚔

Limited Invincibility

Yo! You can earn limited Invincibility in the second mission of *Rambo III*. When you reach the second mission, move up and to the far left from the starting point until you reach the destructible box. Head to the left until a shiny bit of the

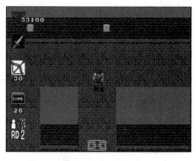

box is showing. Wait until no enemy soldiers are on-screen and then destroy the box with an arrow. At the moment of impact, move left as far as you can with a patch of smoke behind you. Rambo will become indestructible until he reaches the Bonus Stage where bombs, helicopters, or tanks can do him in. Warning: If Rambo destroys any other boxes he'll lose his Invincibility.

Make a Quick Escape

Become a quick escape artist with this prison breakout trick for Round 2 of *Rambo III*. Rescue the two left prisoners first, and then head for the last prisoner in the upper right-hand corner. Once you've rescued him, place bombs in a line down the wall on the left-hand side of the prison cell. When these bombs blow, they'll blast an opening in the wall. Run through the hole to escape with time to spare!

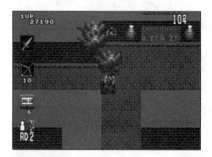
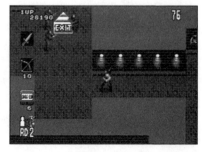

⚔ Ranger-X ⚔

Level Skip

Rocket past any level in *Ranger-X* with this easy level-skip trick. At any time during play, press Start to pause the game. Then press Up, Down, Up, Down, Up, Down, Button C, B, A, Right, and then Left. If you've done the trick correctly,

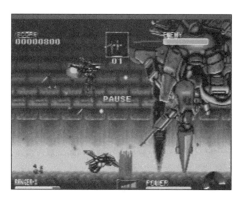

the music should begin again. Then press Button B to make the screen fade and the next level appear. You can keep repeating this trick until you get to the level you want.

★ Revenge of Shinobi ★

Unlimited Shurikens

Shinobi's a slice-and-dice machine with this easy trick you can

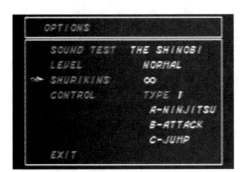

use to earn unlimited Shurikens in *Revenge of Shinobi*. To perform the trick, go to the Options screen and select 00 Shurikens. Wait for 15 seconds; the 00 changes to an infinity symbol. Now your knives are never-ending.

Bust the Rainbow Shot

The Rainbow Shot is your strongest weapon in *Revenge of Shinobi*. To perform this slick Shuriken-tossing trick, press the Jump button and then quickly press Up on the directional pad and hit jump again to somersault. Finally, hit Button B during your somersault and you'll toss eight Shurikens at once. When Shinobi uses this in combination with the Unlimited Shurikens trick above, he's a true master of the martial arts.

Tons of 1-Ups!

Shinobi's tough, but a few extra 1-Ups won't hurt. You can max out on 1-Ups in Round 3-2, the Cargo Jet, of *Revenge of Shinobi*. When you reach the Jet, head for the elevator and go up. Move right on the upper level until you reach the second eleva-

tor. Now, go down and shoot the last box on the upper level. There's a 2-Up in the box. Once you've grabbed the 2-Up, let yourself die! You'll lose a Life, but gain one in the process. Repeat this technique and fill up your Life Line! The counter won't register more than nine, but you can keep earning Extra Lives until you're satisfied.

More 1-Ups!

Pump up your 1-Ups again in the Motor Kill, Round 4-2, of *Revenge of Shinobi*. When you reach Mission 4, move to the edge of the first ledge, jump, and execute a Rainbow Jump. A box with a 2-Up will appear just under the conveyor belt. Jump to grab the
box. You'll die, but earn an Extra Life in the process. Repeat this procedure over and over to earn mucho Lives.

Earn 30,000 Bonus Points

What ninja would turn down 30,000 Bonus Points? One who can't multiply! To earn 30,000 Bonus Points at the end of any round of *Revenge of Shinobi*, you have to finish the level with enough Shurikens to equal 11 times the number of Lives you have remaining. If you can count and fight at the same time, the points are yours.

Escape from the Final Maze

You'd be amazed at how complex the last level of *Revenge of Shinobi* is. Here's our escape route for the Level 8-2 maze: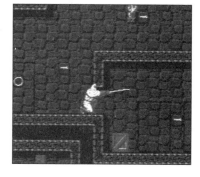

Enter the maze and move to your right, jumping over the first circle door. Head down and to the right into the little lower room and enter the next circle door you reach. Next, enter the circle door immediately to your right. As you go through the door, hold Right on the directional pad to avoid falling into the pit on the other side of the door.

Move right and jump over the first circle door you reach. When you come to a dead end, move left, crouch, and jump into the small opening. Grab all of the Power-Ups in this secret room so you'll be ready to defeat Neo Zeed at the end of the game.

Leave the secret room through the small opening and head up, jumping from wooden platform to wooden platform. At the top, move to your left until you can't proceed any further. Now go up and to the right. Enter the circle door to the far right.

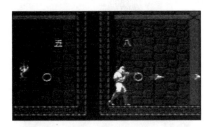

Continue to your right until you reach a wall. Jump over the wall and go through the small opening.

Fall straight down on the other side of the wall in order to avoid landing in the door at the bottom. Jump over the door to the far right and you'll land between two crates.

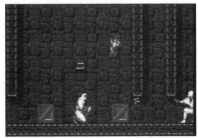

Move left and crouch underneath the walls. Enter the first circle door you reach after you pass the rifle snipers. Now, go left and battle the flying ninjas. Take the far-left bottom door, and you're out of the maze. Time to battle Zeed!

Keep Naoko Alive

Yipes! You gotta finish Neo Zeed fast in *Revenge of Shinobi* or Naoko will get squashed by a cement slab. To save Naoko, jam the gear mechanism of the slab. Stand near the right wall and use a Rainbow Jump. Some of your Shurikens will

hit Zeed and some will jam the gear mechanism of the slab. Listen for a creaking sound to know if you've performed the trick correctly. The wall only stops for two or three seconds, so keep jumping until Zeed is a goner.

Kill Neo Zeed Quickly

Zeed's an ugly dude. Here's the trick to use if you want to kill him fast. First off, stock up on Ninjitsu Magic during Level 8, and save it for Zeed. When you enter the room where you'll battle Neo Zeed, immediately use your Ikazuchi Magic. When Zeed reaches the floor and is ready for battle, kneel next to him and start firing at will. Your Ikazuchi Magic lasts for ten seconds. When you lose it, immediately use the Ikazuchi Magic again, kneel next to Zeed, and continue to fire as rapidly as you can. Zeed's done for in about five more seconds!

☆ Road Rash ☆

Cool Passwords

Use these passwords to begin with the bike of your choice:

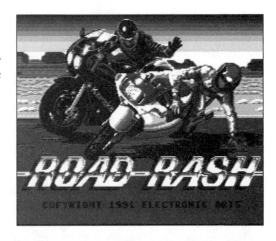

Shuriken 400 (Level 3): 31007 02TO1 007B4 30OME

Panda 600 (Level 1): 10101 02DV1 01GS7 11FKR
Panda 600 (Level 1): 11342 00980 101C1 11HFU
Panda 600 (Level 1): 11312 00BJ0 100LM 11UCI
Panda 600 (Level 3): 31007 02TO0 007TH 31NL2

Banzai 750 (Level 1): 10000 00NE1 011D9 126OU
Banzai 750 (Level 3): 34441 01MS0 NV8UC 3QJ8R
Banzai 750 (Level 3): 31007 02TO1 009FT 32OLD

Kamikaze 750 (Level 1): 10000 00PP1 0109M 13J0J
Kamikaze 750 (Level 3): 31007 02TO0 10BLL 33NM1

Shuriken 1000 (Level 1): 10000 01A61 010N9 14I1J
Shuriken 1000 (Level 3): 31007 02TO1 11CE5 34O1P

Ferruci 850 (Level 1):
10000 01ES0 110G4
15BMT

Ferruci 850 (Level 3):
32673 01R01 011DO
35T7Q

Ferruci 850 (Level 3):
31007 031S1 00824
351EF

Panda 750 (Level 1):
10000 026A0 1132H
16IOA

Panda 750 (Level 3):
32674 02EA1 100ET
36RCN

Panda 750 (Level 3):
31007 031S0 002ET
360DD

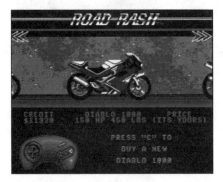

Diablo 1000 (Level 1):
10000 02FM0 101B1
177E9

Diablo 1000 (Level 2):
11145 02T91 110TN
2F9MV

Diablo 1000 (Level 3):
31007 031S1 00115
37176

Diablo 1000 (Level 4):
00000 03231 0100J
479KT

☆ Road Rash II ☆

Begin with Any Bike

Here's a slick trick that'll enable you to begin *Road Rash II* with any bike you like. Begin your game and then go to the Options screen. Select Set Player mode and then

choose Mano a Mano at any level. Then, exit and go to the Bike Shop. Select any bike you'd like. Return to the Options screen and choose Set Player mode again. Next,

choose the type of game you want. Select Take Turns and copy the password. Begin your game and you're racing with the bike of your choice. When it's Player Two's turn, they can choose their bike with the same procedure.

Passwords

Straddle the Diablo 1000N Bike at any level you like with these *Road Rash II* codes:

> **Level 1:** Diablo 1000N Bike, $295,020 - E66T 1ILV
> **Level 2:** Diablo 1000N Bike, $295,020 - E66T 2ILU
> **Level 3:** Diablo 1000N Bike, $295,020 - E66T 3ILP
> **Level 4:** Diablo 1000N Bike, $295,020 - E66T 4ILO
> **Level 5:** Diablo 1000N Bike, $295,020 - E66T 5ILR

Passwords

Or, ride the bike of your choice:

> **Ultra Light**
> **Panda 500:** 0DJ6 12NU
> **Shuriken TT 250:** 0KAU 24MK
> **Panda 900:** 04AC 16NM
> **Banzai 7.11:** 039D 29UQ
>
> **Nitro Class**
> **Banzai 600 N:** 0NRC 2AMS
> **Banzai 750 N:** 05ML 1DN9
> **Shuriken 1000 N:** 01D5 1FNK
> **Banzai 7.11 N:** 08CC 2HUD
> **Diablo 1000 N:** 01HT 2JUQ
>
> **Super Bike**
> **Panda 600:** 0ARL 1KNO
> **Banzai 600:** 08FO 1MNH
> **Banzai 750:** 0HCN 2OMO
> **Shuriken 1000:** 03V5 1RNK
> **Diablo 1000:** 096H 2TM9

✪ Rolling Thunder 2 ✪

Passwords

To avoid gathering moss in *Rolling Thunder 2,* check out these passwords:

Round 1

Level 2: Magical Thunder Learned Secret

Level 3: Natural Fighter Created Genius

Level 4: Rolling Nucleus Smashed Neuron

Level 5: Curious Program Punched Powder

Level 6: Logical Leopard Blasted Secret

Level 7: Private Isotope Desired Target

Level 8: Natural Rainbow Elected Future

Level 9: Magical Machine Muffled Killer

Level 10: Digital Nucleus Punched Device

Level 11: Private Thunder Created Powder

Round 2
Level 1: Rolling Program Smashed Genius
Level 2: Curious Rainbow Learned Future
Level 3: Magical Isotope Blasted Device
Level 4: Private Leopard Punched Neuron
Level 5: Slender Fighter Elected Genius
Level 6: Digital Rainbow Muffled Secret
Level 7: Logical Thunder Smashed Powder
Level 8: Rolling Machine Desired Future
Level 9: Slender Nucleus Blasted Target
Level 10: Curious Isotope Created Killer
Level 11: Natural Program Desired Neuron

✦ Sagaia ✦

Unlimited Continues

Can't get enough of a good thing? No problem! Use this complicated pad trick to earn unlimited Continues in *Sagaia*. When the Title screen appears, press Button B three times, Button C, Button A three times, Button B two times, and Button C three times. If you've performed the trick correctly, the words "Free Play" will appear at the bottom of the screen.

Stage Select

Here's a trick you can use to choose any stage in *Sagaia*. Wait until the Title screen appears and press Button C, Button A, Button C, Button B, Button C, Button A, Button B, Button A, Button B, Button C, Button A, and Button C. If you've performed the trick correctly, the words "Zone Select" will appear at the bottom of the screen.

Sound Test

To hear all of *Sagaia*'s sounds you'll first need to earn a high score in the game. Once you've got a high score, input your initials as "ZZT" on the High Score screen. This sends you to the Sound Test mode!

Super Star Level

If *Sagaia*'s easy for you, check out the expert level. When the Title screen appears, press Button C 12 times. Now, get out there and show 'em your stuff.

✂ Saint Sword ✂

Passwords

Have sword will travel? Use these passwords to check out each of the stages in both chapters of *Saint Sword*:

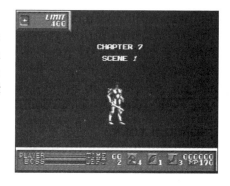

Chapter 1	
Stage 2: HTVO4Y	**Stage 5-2:** R352GM
Stage 3: I1WCUN	**Stage 6:** R2L0CT
Stage 4: J2J0CJ	**Stage 6-2:** TYL0CR
Stage 4-2: N4P2GZ	**Stage 7:** X25DWI
Stage 5: M1MRAE	**Stage 7-2:** Z25ROQ

Chapter 2	
Stage 1: EOFLST	**Stage 5:** O2NQ06
Stage 2: H2KK2R	**Stage 5-2:** R24RMG
Stage 3: K4PVW5	**Stage 6:** U4P2G6
Stage 4: J02ZAY	**Stage 6-2:** W4P2G8
Stage 4-2: L1MZAL	**Stage 7:** Y35F4U
	Stage 7-2: X02CYH

⬙ Shadow Blasters ⬙

Invincibility

There's not a shadow of a doubt that this little two controller trick gives you Invincibility in *Shadow Blasters*. Wait until the Title screen appears and

then choose a two-player game. Select your characters. Once you begin playing, let Player One's energy level drop down to the last block on your life bar. Now, while rapidly pressing Start on Player Two's control pad, let Player One get hit once more. Player One's character will flash in the center of the screen and become invincible. You can repeat this technique for each of your characters. Just remember that you can't pick up energy while you're invincible, although you can pick up everything else.

✴ Shadow Dancer ✴

Practice Level Select

Glide through *Shadow Dancer*'s tough areas with a little pre-fight practice. You can check out any level, except for the boss and bonus areas. Wait until the Title screen appears and then simultaneously press

Buttons A, B, and C, and then press Start. A third option called "Stage Practice" will appear on the Menu screen.

Bonus Round 3-Up

Show them you're not just another ninja by scoring a 3-Up in any bonus round of *Shadow Dancer*. All you have to

do is zap 50 ninjas. The easiest way to do this is to move over to the far left of the screen and fire as rapidly as possible.

Easy Bonus Round 1-Up

If you're feeling lazy, snag an easy 1-Up in any bonus round of *Shadow Dancer*. Just let yourself fall through the bonus round without firing any Shurikens or nailing any ninjas.

A Bunch of 1-Ups

Here are the locations of most of the 1-Ups in *Shadow Dancer*.

Stage 1-2: There's a 1-Up where the second set of debris drops out of the sky and the Roly-Poly sits.

Stage 2-1: There's a 2-Up on the bottom right-hand corner of the bridge.

Stage 2-2: Near the end of the train is a 1-Up. It's above the right side of the last car!

Stage 3-1: To snag a 2-Up, power up and then zap the lone Spinning Warrior on the extreme right side of the ground floor.

Stage 4-1: There's a 1-Up suspended over this pit.

Stage 5-1, Room 3: Try to snag this 1-Up.

Stage 5-1, Room 5: There's a 2-Up above the door at the end of the stage. Jump before entering the door.

50,000 Bonus Points

You'd better like hand-to-sword combat if you want to snag a 50,000 point Bonus in any level of *Shadow Dancer*. You've got to play in the Non-Shuriken mode.

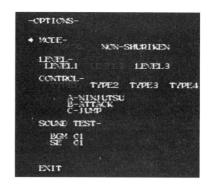

200,000 Extra Points

Use this trick to snag 200,000 Bonus points each time you kill a boss in *Shadow Dancer*. Attack the boss until his defense is down to his last one or two flames. Now, dodge his attack until the clock starts the 10-second countdown. When the clock winds down to the last second, use your ninja magic. The computer will reward you with an extra 200,000 points! This trick works on every boss except for Stavros (the final boss).

◙ Shadow of the Beast II ◙

Game Credits

Check out all of *Shadow of the Beast*'s programmers. Wait until the Psygnosis logo appears, and then simultaneously press and

hold down Buttons A, B, and C, and then press Start. The names of the programmers will appear on-screen.

☯ Shinobi III: Return of the Ninja Master ☯

Invincibility

Zeed can't touch a hair on Shinobi's head when you activate this invincibility trick. When the title screen appears, select the Option mode. Choose

the "Music" option and use Button B to play the following tunes in this order: He Runs, Japonesque, Shinobi Walk, Sakura, and Getufu. Begin your game, and Shinobi's invincible.

Unlimited Shurikens

To snag unlimited Shurikens in *Shinobi III*, go to the Option screen and choose "Shuriken" on Sound Effects, "Shinobi" for Music, and "Shurikens Hits" for Voice. Then, go to "Shuriken," and select 00 as your number. Wait, and the zero will transform to an infinity symbol.

■ Shove It! ■

Last Level Password

We don't want to push you, but you can use this password to check out the last level of *Shove It!*: !AYASAM!

The Simpsons:
★ Bart vs. the Space Mutants ★

NES Magic

NES fans of *Bart vs. the Space Mutants* will find that tricks that work on the NES version of the game also work on the Genesis version. In case you've forgotten the Bartmeister's moves, we've listed a few of our favorite.

3-Up Krusty

Bag three free Lives for bad boy Bart in Level 1 of *Bart vs. the Space Mutants*. Head for the Kwik-E-Mart and launch a bottle rocket at the small "E" in the sign. Catch the Krusty icon as it falls and the Lives are yours.

Sound Test

To check out the sounds of the *The Simpsons*, fire a rocket at the "E" in the Kwik-E-Mart sign in Level 1 of the game. This puts you into the Sound Test mode!

Unlimited Lives

Krusty's crazy Fun House on Level 3 is a great place to score big in *The Simpsons*. After you begin the level, walk into the first building you reach. When you come to the first platform under the air-blowing pipes, stand still. Eventually coins will begin to shoot out at you. You'll earn a 1-Up with every 15 coins. The counter only goes to nine, but you can stand on the platform and earn as many Lives as you like!

Win at the Wheel

In Level 3 of *Bart vs. the Space Mutants* you can fix the odds in Bart's favor at the Wheel of Fortune. Select and use the magnet, and whatever number Bart guesses is always chosen.

☆ Slaughter Sport ☆

Character Select

This *Slaughter Sport* trick's gonna kill you! To choose your favorite fighter in the game, wait until the words "Press Start" appear on the Title screen. Now, use one of the following button press combinations to pick your fighter:

Bonopart: Button A, Up, Button C

Buff: Left, Button C, Button B

El Toro: Simultaneously press Buttons B and C, then Button A, Up

Guano: Up, Right, and then simultaneously press Buttons A and B

M.C. Fire: Down, Button C, Right

Mondu: Simultaneously press Buttons A and B, then Down, Left

Ramses: Right, Left, Button A

Robo Chic: Right, Up, Down

Sheba: Simultaneously press Buttons B and C, Button B, Button B

Skinny: Right, Down, Right

Webra: Simultaneously press Buttons A and C, Up, Right

Weezil: Down, Right, Up

✦ Sol-Deace ✦

Stage Select and 99 Ships

Shoot into the stratosphere with this trick that'll earn you a Stage Select and 99 ships in *Sol-Deace*. During

the Title screen press Button A, Button B, Button C, Button A, Button B, Button C, Button B, Button C, Button B, Button A, and Start. Now you're in the Configuration mode. Move your cursor to the Start input and choose any level in the game. Next, move the cursor to Mode and press Right on your control pad until "MY99" appears on-screen. Now you're armed to the teeth with 99 ships. Exit the menu and choose Continue to begin play.

Skip a Stage!

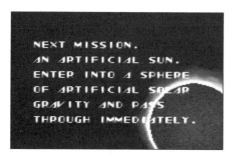

If you're bored with the level you're playing on in *Sol-Deace*, all you have to do is simultaneously press Buttons A, B, and C to skip to the next level.

✸ Sonic the Hedgehog ✸

Level Select

Sonic's even faster than you thought. With this trick you can choose any level in *Sonic the Hedgehog.* During the Title screen

press Up, Down, Left, and Right. If you've performed the trick correctly you'll hear a bell. Finally, hold down Button A and press Start. Choose your level and go!

Debug Mode

Something weird is going on. There's a Debug mode in *Sonic the Hedgehog* that enables you to do some strange things to your game. To activate the Debug mode, wait until the Title screen appears and then press Up, Button C, Down, Button C, Left, Button C, Right, and Button C on Controller 1. Now, simultaneously press Button A and Start until your game begins. Finally, press Button B to enter the Debug mode. Once you're in this mode you can use Button A to select objects and Button C to move and place them.

Speedy Sonic Demo

Sonic can run even faster than normal during the Demo mode of the game with this easy trick. All you have to do is simultaneously press and hold Buttons A, B, and C during the Demo mode. When you release the buttons, Sonic will go nuts! This trick also works during the game's end credits. For a special surprise, grab the Invincibility monitor!

Easy Emerald Collection

Use this trick to snag all of the Emeralds before Sonic even starts his mission. Go to the Level Select mode, select the Special Stage and try to grab the first Emerald. If you manage to grab the Emerald, advance to the end of the Special Stage, and wait until the Emerald appears. Next, reset the game and again choose Special Stage. Press Start and go for the second Emerald. At the end of the Special Stage, the game should indicate that you

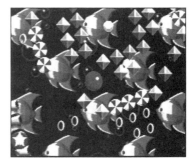

have two Emeralds. Repeat this procedure until you have all six Emeralds. Finally, go through the Special Stage one last time to try to earn a Continue and maybe a 1-Up. Wait at the end of the Special Stage until Stage 1 begins, and play a regular game. Now beat Sonic and you'll see an all-new ending. Note: You can't get to the Special Stage during the game.

Make Tunnels at Dead Ends

Sonic's got a nifty move that enables him to make tunnels in areas that seem like dead ends, such as in the Starlight Zone, Act 1. Look for these rooms in places where the walls or cliffs have a different, rough texture. Run straight at the wall and just before you reach it, push Down to use your Super Sonic Spin Attack. This blasts Sonic through the wall and he can collect whatever goodies are hidden on the other side.

1-Ups, Hidden Rooms, and Rings and Things

Here's a few 1-Ups that'll make *Sonic the Hedgehog* a little easier to master. There's a basic strategy you can use when hunting for 1-Ups that makes it easy to rack up lots of Extra Lives. In any level where you can earn three or four 1-Ups, grab them all and then die before you reach the end of the level. You'll lose one Life but keep the others you gathered. Now you can replay the level and gather more Lives. Repeat this procedure until you have as many lives as you want.

Green Hill Zone

Act 1-1: When you reach the first platform with a Super Ring monitor, jump into the tree just to the right of the platform. Use the hidden spring to reach a secret cache of Rings.

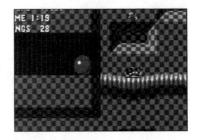

Act 1-2: Use Sonic's wall-crashing technique just to the left of the Power Sneaker. Inside this secret room you'll find two Super Rings and a Shield.

Act 1-2: Go left past the Power Sneaker on the lower path. You'll pass two Springs. Bounce up to the left and you'll reach a red spring. Jump on the red spring and veer slightly to the left as you fall. If you're lucky, you'll land

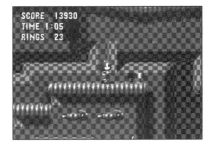

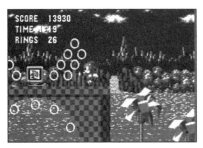

the bridge and then leap to grab the 1-Up.

Act 1-3: You'll find another hidden room to blast through at the right end of the lower path.

Act 1-3: There's another secret hidden room with a 1-Up in this act. Advance Sonic until he reaches a solid wall (where you can't move ahead without using the bumper). Use the Tunnel technique to blast Sonic through the wall to a secret speed tunnel.

on the top of the loop where you can snag mucho Rings and a 1-Up.

You can also snag this 1-Up by using the Power Sneaker. Once you've strapped them on make a running start from

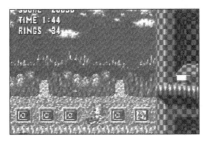

Keep moving ahead without jumping on any bumpers. When you reach the area with the blue water background, you'll find six monitors at the base of the waterfall.

Act 1-3: Look for a series of floating ledges to the right of a high lamppost. When you find the ledges, jump on the second one to the right of the post, and then fall straight down.

With luck you'll land on top of the loop where you can snag a 1-Up.

Marble Zone

Act 2-2: There's a hidden room just next to the lava pit with a group of lava spouts. Usually you would jump up to continue. Instead, run and jump on the single block resting against the left side of the wall.

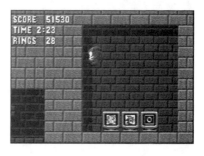

You'll blast into a secret room. Inside this hidden room you'll find two Super Rings and a 1-Up.

Act 2-3: Look for a spiked weight with a space to its right where Sonic can stand. Slip into the space where the weight falls and blast through the wall to the left. Inside you'll find a hidden room with a 1-Up. P.S.—To escape, you can either go back the way you came, or jump up.

Spring Yard Zone

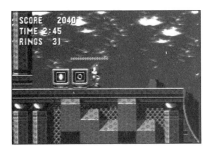 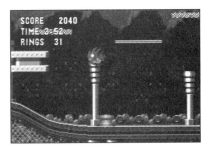

Act 3-1: For tons of Power-Ups, look for the button and platform near the beginning of the Act. Jump on the button and
climb on-board the platform
to ride to a special area.

Act 3-1: There's a hidden
tunnel in the first shaft after
the tunnel lamppost. Hold
right as you jump off the yel-
low bumper and you'll enter a
secret Ring tunnel.

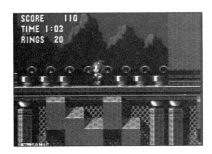 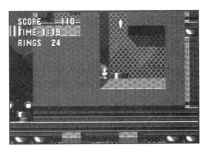

Act 3-2: To discover a hidden Ring tunnel in this Act, look for
a group of six red bumpers and jump on the one to the far
right, while holding right. You'll enter a secret tunnel with a
bumper that shoots you to a Ring shaft.

Act 3-2: As you move along the lower path of this Act, you'll reach two red bumpers. Jump on the one to the right and hold right to land in a hidden tunnel. Inside you'll find Rings and a 1-Up.

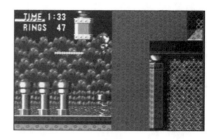

Act 3-3: Jump on the red bumper to the left of the second lamppost. Run up until you reach a floating platform. Use the floating platforms to reach a green ledge. Next, move to the right and blast through the wall to enter a secret tunnel. Inside you'll find a 1-Up and a Shield.

Act 3-3: When you reach the pinball area, use the ramp to run around and to the right. As you reach the right-hand side, hold Right on your control pad and you'll enter a secret room.

Labyrinth Zone

Act 4-2: There's a giant room in this Act that seems to have no entrance. To gather the goodies, all you have to do is look for the door button that's hidden behind a video monitor. It's hidden behind one of

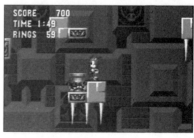

the monitors on the ledges above the water.

Act 4-3: In this Act there's a secret room to the right of the tidal wave area. To reach the tidal wave, fall down the hole in the middle of four spikes.

After the tidal wave, move to the right. When you reach an area with lots of ledge and pulleys, search the left wall to find the secret room. The door is open, but you'll have to enter the room by falling from above. Inside you'll find four Super Rings and a 1-Up.

Star Light Zone

Act 5-1: Grab the 1-Up at the start of this zone, run a little ways down the ramp, and then back up. This clears the blocks around the 1-Up.

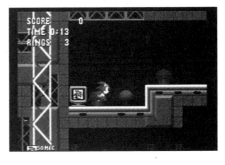

Act 5-2: Reaching the 1-Up in this Act is pretty tricky. From the beginning, head right until you come to the collapsing ledges. Jump down the hole left by the ledges and move to the right. When you reach an area with floating ledges and a ramp to the right, take the ramp. When you see another ramp above you, jump on it and eventually you'll reach a Super Ring, Invincibility Monitor, and a 1-Up.

Act 5-3: Use the ramps and catapults to stay in the middle of this Act and you'll easily spot a 1-Up. Use a catapult to bounce left into a secret room.

Scrap Brain Zone

Act 6-2: There's a 1-Up along the upper path in this act.
Act 6-3: If you keep moving to the left in each area of this Act, you'll eventually reach a 1-Up. It's hidden in a room to the far left of the Act.

✳ Sonic the Hedgehog 2 ✳

Stage Select

Choosing any stage you like in *Sonic 2*'s a snap. Go to the Options screen, and then select the Sound Test box. Use Button B to play the following sounds in this order: 19, 65, 9, 17. If you've performed the trick correctly, you'll hear a ringing sound at the beginning of sound 17. Press Start, and wait

until the Title screen appears. Then, press and hold Button A and then press Start again. When the Stage Select screen appears, use the cursor to highlight any stage, even the Death Egg Stage, and press Start to begin your game.

Instant Golden Sonic

There's another Sound Test trick that enables you to begin play at any stage with all the Chaos Emeralds already collected! Perform the Stage Select trick above, and then

use the cursor to highlight the new Sound Test. Play the following sounds in this order: 4, 1, 2, 6. Begin your game at any level, and then collect 50 Rings. Once you've grabbed the Rings, you'll transform into the Golden Sonic.

↟ Space Harrier II ↟

Level Select

Cool! You can hurl through *Space Harrier II* with this stage skipper. Hit Start and wait until the screen that says "Stuna Area" appears. Next, push Left or Right to choose any level. But remember, you can't complete the game if you begin with one of the later levels. If you want to end the game you must start from the beginning.

✦ Space Invaders '91 ✦

Round Select

Strap on your helmet, space jockeys. You can choose any round with this trick for *Space Invaders '91*. Wait until the Title screen appears, then simultaneously press and hold Buttons A and

C, and press Start. The game will pause as the Title screen

fades, and then the first level appears. During the pause press Button B, Button A, and Button C. A round Select screen will appear. Choose your level and go get 'em.

⊕ Spider-Man ⊕

Power-Up Code

Spidey's a snap when you use this code to power-up your Webs and Life, have limited Invincibility, and even skip levels. Go to the game's Option screen, move the cursor to Level, and set it to Spidey. Then, press and hold Start on Controller 2

and then simultaneously press and hold Buttons A, B, and C on Controller 1. While continuing to hold all these buttons, press Up and Right on Controller 1. If you did the trick correctly, three exclamation marks will appear next to the difficulty setting. Once the code is in place you can pause the game any time during play and press Button A to fill your web, Button B to fill your Life, and Button C for five seconds of Invincibility. Simultaneously press Buttons A, B, and C to skip a level.

Battle Venom

Here's a poisonous trick that enables you to battle Venom in the first level. Choose Nightmare mode, begin the first level, and then crawl through the crates just past the attacking German Shep-

herd. Keep moving to your right and you'll battle Venom near the forklift.

Level 4 Power-Up

If you're low on Life by the time you reach Level 4 of *Spider-Man*, use this slick trick to power up. When you reach Level 4, head for the apartment. Enter it, and then quickly leave again. You're sent to the beginning of the level. Now, proceed and grab the Life Power-Up in the Tree. Repeat this procedure until your Life is maxed! Psst . . . this trick works anywhere there's a Power-Up, especially towards the beginning of a level!

Fight Four Bosses at Once

If your Spidey senses are tingling for the fight of your Life, you can battle four bosses at once in the last level of the game. When you reach Electro after Level 6, don't move in for the kill. Instead, keep moving in the direction of the Bomb. In fact, don't fight any of the bosses you encounter along the way — just keep moving towards the Bomb. Eventually you'll have Electro, Lizard, Hobgoblin, and Venom all on your tail. Now's your chance to really show off your web-slinging skills!

 Splatterhouse 2 ✳

Passwords

Slash through *Splatterhouse* with these level passwords:

> **Level 2:** EDK NAI ZOL LDL
> **Level 3:** IDO GEM IAL LDL
> **Level 4:** ADE XOE ZOL OME
> **Level 5:** EFH VEI RAG ORD
> **Level 6:** ADE NAI WRA LKA
> **Level 7:** EFH XOE IAL LDL
> **Level 8:** EDK VEI IAL LDL

✦ Starflight ✦

Unlimited Endurium

Soar into riches with this trick that earns you unlimited Endurium in *Starflight*. First, fly to Sphexi. Sphexi is the home world of the Veloxi and is located at 132,165. Land at 45N X 17E. Pick up the Endurium and the Crystal Orb. Blast off and then land again at the same coordinates. Repeat this procedure until you have all the Endurium you need.

⊕ Steel Empire ⊕

Round Select

Soar to any round in *Steel Empire* just by swapping a few numbers on the Options screen. Enter the Options screen, and then highlight the Sound Test selection. Play the following sounds in this order: Sound 1 twice, Sound 9 once, and Sound 2 twice. After you've played the sounds, a Round Entry option will appear on-screen. Highlight it, and use Left and Right on your control pad to change the numbers to the round of your choice.

☆ Stormlord ☆

Skip Levels

If the weather looks bad, use this easy trick to skip any level in *Stormlord*. To advance to the next level, simply hit Pause, Button C, Button B three times, Button A four times, Button C two times, and Button A four times. You

can repeat this procedure any time during the game.

Nine Extra Lives

Here's a trick that you can use to get nine Extra Lives in *Stormlord*. When you're running low on spare Lives, pause the game and press Button A four times, Button C two times, Button B three times, Button C, and Button A. You can do this trick as many times as you like anywhere in the game!

More Time

If you're running out of time on any level in *Stormlord*, you can use this trick to turn back the clock. Pause the game and then press Button B, Button A three times, Button C, Up three times, and Button A three times. Use this trick as often as necessary.

 Street Fighter II Special Champion Edition

Turn Off All Normal Moves in the One-Player Mode!

Make your Street Fightin' a little more interesting. You'll need a six-button controller for this code. When the Capcom logo appears, press Down, Button Z, Up, Button X, Button A, Button Y, Button B, Button C on Controller One. If the trick worked, you'll hear a chime.

Now you can use your special techniques!

Fight at Five-Star Speed in Champion Mode!

Speed things up with this super code. Instead of pressing Start, wait for the opening cinematic sequence to appear. As the buildings in the background of the blue *Street Fighter II* logo start to fade, press Down, Button Z, Up, Button X, Button A, Button Y, Button B,

and Button C on Controller One. If the code worked, you'll hear a chime. When the Title Screen appears, you can choose up to five stars of speed in Champion Mode.

Character vs. Same Character in Battle Mode!

Get ready to see double, 'cause you can fight your mirror image in the Battle mode. When screen appears which enables you to choose either Match Play or Elimination Rules in the Battle mode, push Down, Button Z, Up, Button X, Button A, Button Y, Button B, and Button C

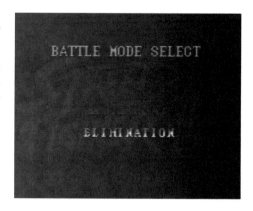

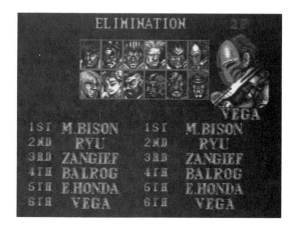

on Controller Two. If the code worked, you'll hear a chime.

When the Battle Mode begins, you can choose the same World Warrior for both players!

✷ Streets of Rage ✷

Double Your Chances

If you're having a tough time getting through the *Streets of Rage* on your own, try this trick. Begin your game as Axel. When things get tough and Axel's near the end, you can hit Start on Controller 2. Player Two will join the game as Adam. This gives you a few more chances to beat the game.

Second Ending

There's a second ending in *Streets of Rage*. To check it out play in the two-player mode until you reach the Syndicate Leader. The boss will ask you to join his gang. Have one of the players answer "yes" and the other "no." Since one of the heroes

betrayed the police force, they end up facing off against each other to control the streets.

✸ Streets of Rage 2 ✸

Play As the Same Character

No, you're not seeing double. This controller trick enables both players in a two-player *Streets of Rage 2* battle to fight as the same character. Wait until the Title screen appears, and then press and hold down Button B and Right on Controller 1, and Button A and Left on Controller 2. Continue to hold all of these buttons, and then press Button C on Controller 2.

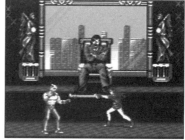

Round Select and More

Punch in this *Streets of Rage* code to choose any round, begin with 27 Lives, and even play hidden difficulty levels, including Mania. Wait until the Title screen appears, and

then select Option. Next, on Controller 2, simultaneously press Buttons A and B and then hit Start.

ꙮ Strider ꙮ

Get Permanent Dipodal Saucers

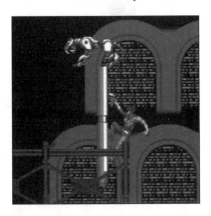

If *Strider*'s feeling lonely, use this trick to get him two permanent robot companions. Grab two robots, just as you normally would—two blocks of your Life bar should become red. Continue to play until you reach a container with the Robo-Panther. Open the container, but don't grab it! Next, take a hit on purpose so that you lose a Robot. Now, touch the Robo-Panther. Continue to play and the Robo-Panther will eventually go away. You'll be left with two Robots who you'll only lose if you fall off the screen or use a Continue.

Just for Fun

Just for fun, check out the hidden panda in Round 3 of *Strider*. To see it, fall to the bottom of the Ballog, just past the huge cannon. Next, move to the left until you reach several ledges with bombs on them.

When you blow up the bombs on the highest ledge, a Panda appears!

Special Music

Get down with *Strider*'s secret Level 4 tune! To hear it, go to the large tree trunk with the vine on the ground just before you fight Lago the Mechanical Dinosaur. To activate the secret tune, move *Strider* very slowly from the left side to the right side of the tree trunk by pressing Right little by little until the music changes. If this trick doesn't work the first time, try again.

Secret Room

Look for a secret room just inside of the reactor in Level 5 of *Strider*. The entrance is next to where you're first upside down. Inside you'll have to battle a couple of wild women, but you can snag a Power-Up.

Laser Fake Out

If you stand in just the right spot, you can avoid damage from the lasers in the second reactor in Level 5 of *Strider*. The trick is to stand so that the capsule on the ground to your left just touches your foot. If you're in the right spot the lasers will pass

right through your body without inflicting any damage!

⚅ Super Hang-On ⚅

Another Options Mode

Cut yourself some slack in *Super Hang-On* with this trick that sends you to an Options menu. You select the game's difficulty, time, language (English or Japanese), and even hear a sound test. Simultaneously press Button A and Start during the Title screen and you're in the Cheat mode!

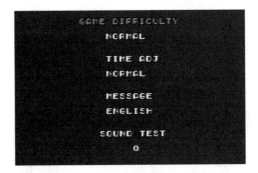

Passwords

Cruise through *Super Hang-On* with these passwords:

> **Jose Alverez, 0 wins, 0 losses, $34,400:**
> 69F1A122F05101
> DFJNCG9D6DJEHW
>
> **Marie Lefoure, 0 wins, 0 losses, $135,300**
> 5723B345135242
> BCKMCG9D7DDQNL

Another Ending Password

Here's a password that enables you to check out the game's ending. All you have to do is dethrone King Arthur in the Original mode and then enter this password:

6FF3F546F35564

FFOSLPIMFJEDGH

Begin the Arcade Mode with a Totally Souped-up Bike

If you're ready to ride, use this password to begin *Super Hang-On*'s Arcade mode with a totally souped-up bike. Once you've entered the code, select Arcade mode and you're ready to roll:

6FF3F546F35564

FFOSLPIMFJEDGH

☆ Super Hydlide ☆

Quick Experience

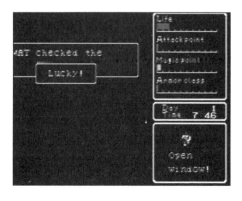

Hum a tune as you rack up mucho Experience Points in *Super Hydlide*. Your game begins in the City of the Forest. Go to the screen with the lake and a bridge. Stand at the bottom of the lake to the left of the bridge and Search. You'll get the message "I found nothing." Don't give up! Try to use your money (it won't work) and then try to Search again. This time the word "Lucky" will appear on-screen and you'll score 30 free Experience Points. And guess what? You really are lucky because you can repeat this procedure as many times as you like!

Sound Test

To check out the sounds of *Super Hydlide*, you're gonna have to do a little traveling. At the beginning of the game, leave the City of the Forest and head left until you reach a small building. Inside, you can listen to the game's sounds.

P.S. Do not forget to

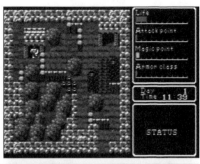

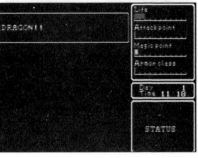

search the building—there's $10,000 just waiting for you!

Instant Replay

If you've managed to beat *Super Hydlide*, you might just feel like checking out the ending one more time. No problem! Begin your game again, leave the City of the Forest, and go to the left until you reach the small building where you received $10,000. Enter the building to the right and you can replay the game's finale.

🚁 Super Thunder Blade 🚁

Avoid Enemy Fire

If you're feeling gun-shy, use this trick to avoid enemy fire in Levels 1, 2,

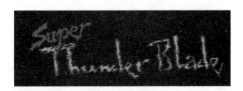

and 3 of *Super Thunder Blade*. Wait until the Title screen appears, and then enter the Options menu. Set the game's difficulty to Hard. Exit the Options screen and begin

your game. Finally, bank to the upper right- or left-hand corner of the screen. If you stay in this spot, you'll be untouchable!

⊕ Super Volleyball ⊕

Special Moves

Serve it up with these super moves for *Super Volleyball*. To perform a Super Serve, simultaneously press Button A, Button B, and Up. To nail a Super Spike that'll knock over anyone on the opposite team who tries to return it, simultaneously press Button A, Button B, and Down after setting your spike.

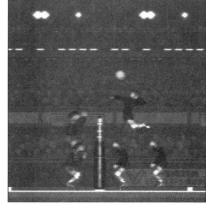

Sword of Sodan

Warp

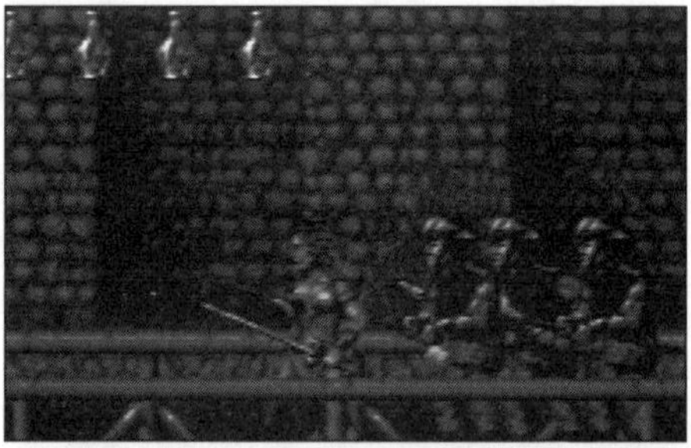

To warp in *Sword of Sodan*, snag four Etherium potions. Gulp them down and you'll zoom ahead a level!

Another Warp

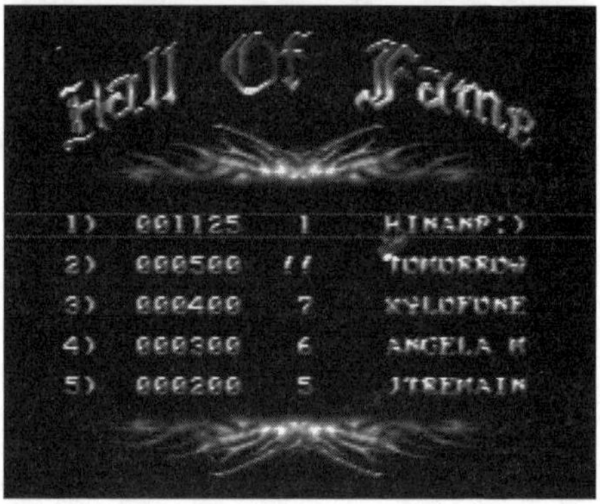

Here's a two-controller warp trick for *Sword of Sodan*. First, earn the top score on the high scores list. Then, instead of entering your name for the high score, enter: HINANP:). Finally, press Start on Controller 2 to skip levels.

Good Potion Notions

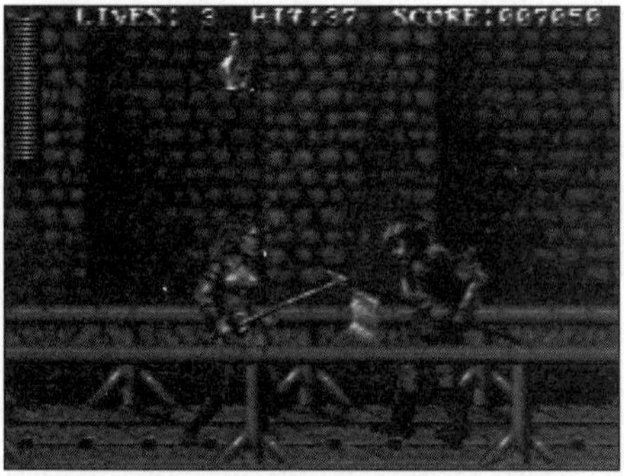

Here are a few potion combos that'll help you take the edge off *Sword of Sodan*:

> **For a Level 1, Level 2, or Level 3 1-Up:**
> Combine a red and a purple potion.

For a Shield: Combine a blue and a purple potion.
For a Flame Sword: Combine an orange and a red potion, or an orange and a purple potion.
For a Zap that kills everything on-screen: Combine a purple, a blue, and an orange potion.

Bad Potion Notions

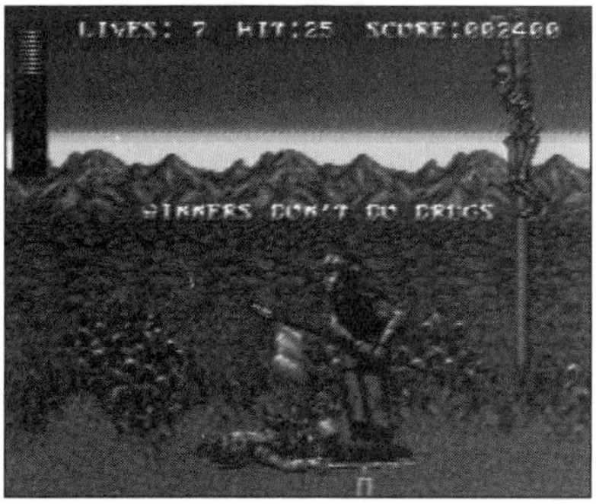

Here are a few potion combos to avoid:

Decreases Your Health: Combine a blue and an orange potion.
Instant Death: Combine a red, a purple, an orange, and a blue potion.

Sword of Vermilion

Sound Test

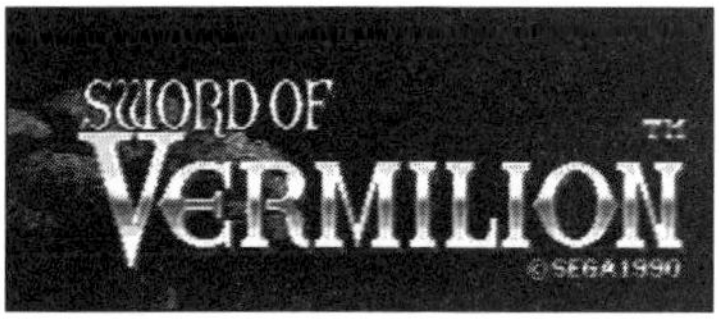

Use this trick to hear all of *Sword of Vermilion*'s sounds and even view a color test. To reach the Selection screen, simultaneously press Buttons A, B, and C on Controller 2 and then hit Start.

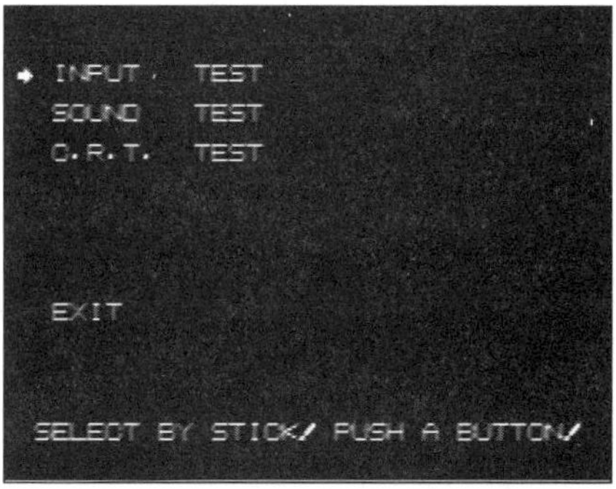

★ Syd of Valis ★

Untouchable Swimming Suit

Here's a change of pace for Yuko in *Syd of Valis*. Wait until the Title screen appears and then press Up, Down, Left, Right, Button A, Button B, Up, Down, and Start on

your control pad. If you've done the trick correctly you'll hear a sound. When you begin your game, Yuko will be wearing a snazzy swim suit which makes her invincible!

No Background Music

Tired of the music? It's easy to get rid of it, even without using "mute" on your remote control. Simply wait until the Title screen appears and then simultaneously press Button B and Start. Every time you die the music will return.

⚔ T2: The Arcade Game ⚔

Stage Select

It's hasta la vista baby when you use this Stage Select code to zap to any part of *T2* you like. Wait until the Title screen appears, and then press Up, Down, Left, Right,

Up, Down, Left, and then Right. If you've done the trick cor-

rectly, you'll hear the word "Excellent." When your game begins, press Start to pause play, and then simultaneously press Buttons B and C to skip to the next stage. Repeat this trick until you reach the stage you want to play on.

Hunter Killer Clues

Nail the Hunter Killers the easy way by memorizing which side of the screen they appear from:

> **1st Plane:** Comes from the left side of the screen.
> **2nd Plane:** Comes from the right side of the screen.

3rd: Left	**10th:** Left	**17th:** Right
4th: Right	**11th:** Right	**18th:** Left
5th: Right	**12th:** Right	**19th:** Right
6th: Left	**13th:** Left	**20th:** Left
7th: Right	**14th:** Right	**21st:** Left
8th: Left	**15th:** Left	**22nd:** Right
9th: Left	**16th:** Left	**23rd:** Left

⊕ Target Earth ⊕

Nine Continues

To begin *Target Earth* with nine Continues, begin your game and play until Rex destroys the space ship. Have Rex die on his way to the shuttle.

Now, choose the Option mode and change pad reset from "Cancel" to "Enable." Stay in the Option mode and hit Button C and Start simultaneously. If you've done the trick correctly, a girl will appear onscreen and award you with nine Continues.

Leave the Option mode and get ready to blast off.

Infinite Continues

Use this variation of the Nine Continue trick to continue infinitely. Begin your game normally, and play to Level 2, or

any level past Level 1. Next, let yourself die. Select the Options screen and hit Start. The girl will appear with the words "Continue Up." When you exit the Options screen, you'll see that you have nine Continues. Continue to play the game, and repeat this procedure whenever you have less than three Continues left! You're set!

Invincibility

It's easy to become invincible in *Target Earth*. Just hit Start on Controller 2. Now you'll live forever.

Two Player Option

There's a strange hidden two-player option in *Target Earth*. To activate it, begin Level 1 and continue to play normally until you

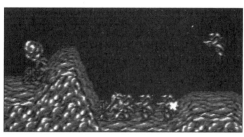

reach the first green alien robot. Now, press Start on Controller 2. This enables one of the players in a two-player game to use the enemies' robot while you still control the regular robot!

Swap Firing Set-Ups

To change your firing set-up in *Target Earth*, simultaneously press Buttons A, B, and C.

Weapons Bonanza

To earn all the weapons on the first level of *Target Earth*, you have to destroy the warship at least 52 miles before the base. But wait, it's even more complicated than that! On your way to the warship you cannot destroy any other enemies! If you perform the trick correctly you'll have 2,800 points and no bonus weapons. When you begin Stage 2, you'll discover that you've been awarded all of the weapons!

Rotate the Title Screen

This trick is just for fun. You can rotate and resize the company logo in *Target Earth*. Using Controller 2, simultaneously press Buttons A, C, and Up and Right on the control pad and the logo will begin to move!

✈ Task Force Harrier ✈

Debug Mode

Debug *Task Force Harrier*'s action with this deadly trick. Press and hold Button A, then turn the power on. When the Title screen appears, release Button A and press Up, Down, Left, Right, Button A, Button B, Button A, Button C, and Button B on your control pad. Select "Config" and you'll discover that the Option mode has new options. "Muteki" is Invincibility and "Window" changes the screen size. To skip any level, press Start to pause the game and then press Button A.

☻ Taz-Mania ☻

Unlimited Continues

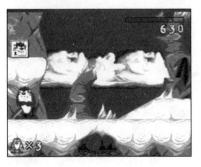

There's an easy way to snag as many Continues as you like in *Taz-Mania*. Head to the second section of the Badlands. Climb to the highest ledge and then walk to the far left until you see a 1-Up. Grab the 1-Up, and then move right until you reach a Rock Monster. Jump off the monster's head to leap up and grab a 3-Up. Cross the bridge until you reach several Bombs. Chow down on the Bombs until you're history. When you begin the level again, repeat this same procedure over and over until you've got as many 1-Ups as you like.

Level Skip, Invincibility, and Level Select

Taz won't have any more tantrums when he sees what you can do with this super trick. Plug in two controllers. When the Title screen appears, simultaneously press Buttons A, B, C, and Start on both controllers. Now you're ready to activate any of the three options.

To skip a level, press Start to pause any time during your game. Then, simultaneously press Buttons A, B, and C on Controller 1. You'll automatically advance to the next level.

To become invincible, press Start to pause your game any time during play. Then, press Button B. Return to your game,

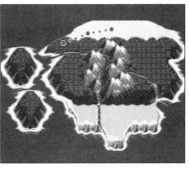

and you're invincible. To turn off the Invincibility, press Start to pause your game again, and then simply press Button A.

To choose any level, press Start once again to pause your game. Then, press Button C. Numbers will appear below the word "Pause." Use Left and Right on your control pad to select any level. When you've reached the level you want, un-pause. You'll zap straight to the level you choose.

• Team USA Basketball •

Passwords

It's a slam dunk when you hit the courts with these *Team USA Basketball* passwords:

> **Play as Team USA in the final game**
> **against the Netherlands:** #XT7RB6
> **See the Closing Ceremonies:** #WT7RDC
>
> **Play as Team USA in the final game**
> **against Lithuania:** FNT7RBQ
> **See the Closing Ceremonies:** FMT7RCO

★ Technocop ★

Power-Up

Use this slick trick to restore your life in *Technocop*. In any building scene, press Start to pause your game. Next, press Button C ten times, Button A five times, Button B two times, and Button A ten times. Now,

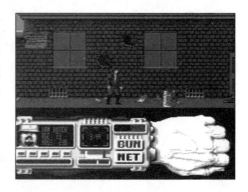

press Start to un-pause. If you've performed the trick correctly, you'll hear the word "Technocop."

Teenage Mutant Ninja Turtles:
❋ The Hyperstone Heist ❋

Stage Select

Cowabunga! Use this trick to choose any stage you like in *Hyperstone Heist*. Wait for the Konami logo to appear on-screen, then press Button C, Button B two times, Button A three times, Button B, and Button C before the logo disappears. Next, press Start.

When the Title screen appears, press Button A, Button B two times, Button C three times, Button B, and finally Button A. Press Start again. An Option screen will appear that enables you to choose any stage.

✗ The Terminator ✗

Sneak Preview

Go ahead and make Arnold's day. To check out the two intro screens without any text, just press and hold Up on the control pad before the screens appear.

✦ Thunder Force II ✦

Level Select

Blast straight to any level in *Thunder Force II* by simultaneously pressing and holding Buttons A, B, and C while turning the power on. Continue to hold the buttons and hit Start when the Title screen appears. Use the screen that appears to choose your starting level, difficulty, and several other options.

Safe Passage

There are lots of dangerous enemies gunning for the Exceliza in *Thunder Force II*, but there are a few ships that you don't have to worry about. The Exceliza is invincible to the Power-Up ships that drop weapons in both the vertical and horizontal stages of the game. Take advantage of this invincibility, especially in the horizontal stages when dodging enemy bullets gets really tough.

Bonus Points

In *Thunder Force II*, you're gonna earn Bonus points depending on how quickly you destroy the four enemy bases in any of the vertical stages. Here's the rundown:

Bonus	Time
250,000 points	Under 1 minute
100,000 points	Under 2 minutes
50,000 points	Under 3 minutes
20,000 points	Under 4 minutes
0 points	Over 5 minutes

In the horizontal stages you'll earn Bonus points based on how many enemies you destroy:

Number of Enemies Destroyed	Bonus Points
200+	100,000
150+	50,000
100+	20,000
50+	10,000

✦ Thunder Force III ✦

Bye-Bye Ending Sequence

Here's a nifty trick that enables you to have some fun with the ending sequence of *Thunder Force III*. During the end sequence, press Button C to make your character's hands wave and eyes wink!

♣ Thunder Fox ♣

Stage Select and Nine Continues

Arm yourself with nine Continues and a stage select with this *Thunder Fox* trick. Wait until the Title screen appears and then push Start to go to the game select screen. Go to the Configuration mode and move the cursor to Music Select. Now, press Button A 13 times. Next, move the cursor to Sound Select and then press Button A 24 times. Finally, move the cursor to Exit and then press Button A, then Button B, and then Button C. Use Button A to choose levels and add Continues.

Tiny Toon Adventures:
⬦ Buster's Hidden Treasure ⬦

Passwords

Bust Tiny Toons with this complete set of passwords:

Dizzy Devil: BYBG LDDL LDBD DLDD LDTG
Calamity Coyote: GRBB TLLD LLBB MILL DLPD
Plucky Duck: XHBQ HZGL LDBQ HZDD LLGM
Fight Toxic Revenger: GJBQ HZZG LLBQ HZZL DDMR
Fight Pirate Ship: QJBW HZZB DLBW HZZK LLMG
Hamton: KTBQ HZZQ WGBQ HZZQ QDVR
End: PDBW HZZQ ZKBQ HZZW ZGJN

☆ ToeJam & Earl ☆

Quick Power-Up

Hey rapmasters! The two star-hoppin' dudes from outer space, ToeJam & Earl, can boogie to higher energy with this trick. During a two-player game, arm both ToeJam & Earl with either the Sling Shot or the Tomatoes. Toss Tomatoes at each other. ToeJam & Earl will snag them and munch them down, filling their energy bit by bit. Keep chowing till you've got full energy.

Sneak Up on Santa

Didn't think you could ever grab Santa? All you have to do is tip-toe up to him. If he looks up, freeze until he looks back in his bag. Then, tip-toe towards him some more. If you manage to grab him before he flies away, he'll drop Christmas presents for you.

Secret Level

Don't be a dufus. Check out Level Zero in *ToeJam & Earl*. Use the Icarus Wings, the Rocket Skates, or the Inner Tube to go all the way to the lower left portion of the map on Level 1.

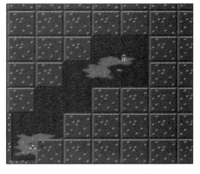

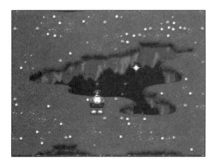

You'll discover an island with a hole in the middle of it. Drop into the hole to reach Level Zero.

On Level Zero you'll find a Lemonade Stand and a snazzy Hot Tub that is complete with Wahines. To receive a 1-Up go to the Lemonade Stand, push Up on your control pad, and then drink the Lemonade.

To power-up your Life Bar, hop into the Hot Tub by standing next to it and pushing Left or Right on your control pad. Hang out in the hot tub until you're fully powered and then jump off the edge of the island. You'll return to the highest level you've reached in the game.

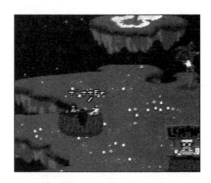

Extra Island on Level 1

Jam your way to the hidden island in the upper right-hand corner of the first level of *Toe-Jam & Earl*. To reach the island, use the Icarus Wings, the Innertube, or the Rocket Skates. The island has some

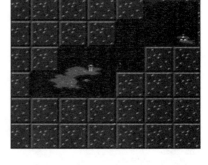

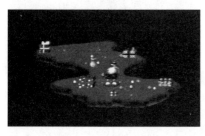

cool presents on it, including an Un-fall, which will transport you back to the highest level you've reached in the game.

Going Up

Here's a quick guide to the location of the Elevators on each level of the Fixed World of *ToeJam & Earl*:

Level 1: Look in the upper right-hand corner of the world.

Level 2: When you're ready to go up, head toward the end of the road in the upper right of the world.

Level 3: Boogie to the left side of the world and look in a large field.

Large 4: In this world, look next to the lake on the bottom left.

Large 5: Go to the end of the road that leads to the bottom left.

Level 6: Head to the upper right in this world.

Level 7: Look next to the lake, in the lower left-hand area.

Level 8: Head to the lower right-hand area of this world.

Level 9: Go to the middle to left lower area of this world.

Level 10: Hope you're shipshape. On this level you'll need to go to the island in the middle of a lake.

Level 11: In this level, go to the lower right-hand corner of the world.

Level 12: Head to the upper right area of this world.

Level 13: Go to the upper right area of this world.

Level 15: You'll need to go to the lower left part of this world.

Level 16: Waddle up to the top middle area of this world.

Level 17: Look just to the right of the center of the world.

Level 18: Head to the top left part of this world.

Level 19: In this world, go to the lower right area of the world.

Level 20: Go to the upper right section of this world.

Level 21: It's also in the upper right part of this world.

Level 22: Head to the upper left area of this world.

Level 23: Ahoy, check out this world's island in the middle of the lake.

Level 24: Look in the upper left area of this world.

Find the Ship Pieces

Here's where to send those rapmasters, ToeJam & Earl, to look for each of the 10 ship pieces in the Fixed World:

Level 2: Look in the lower part of the world, between the left and middle areas.

Level 6: In this world, look in the lower middle area.

Level 10: Check out the upper area of this world, between the middle and right sections.

Level 12: Go to the lower middle area of the world.

Level 15: Look in the upper left section of this world.

Level 17: In this world, look in the upper right area.

Level 20: Go to the lower left part of this world.

Level 21: Check out the lower right area of this world.

Level 23: Look in the upper middle section of this world.

Level 25: Go to the lower right corner of this world for the last piece.

○ Tommy Lasorda Baseball ○

World Series Password Creation

Step up to the plate with these World Series codes that'll do Tommy proud:

> H_ _ flmnjia VXhLQZPqBCVA

Input one of the following letters in the first blank to choose your team:

D - Detroit	**Q** - Texas
E - Toronto	**R** - St. Louis
F - Milwaukee	**S** - New York Mets
G - New York Yankees	**T** - Montreal
H - Boston	**U** - Philadelphia
I - Baltimore	**V** - Pittsburgh
J - Cleveland	**W** - Chicago Cubs
K - Minnesota	**X** - San Francisco
L - Kansas City	**Y** - Cincinnati
M - Oakland	**Z** - Houston
N - Seattle	**a** - Los Angeles
O - Chicago White Sox	**b** - Atlanta
P - California	**c** - San Diego

Use the second blank to choose the opposing team. Just select one letter later in the alphabet than the team's regular letter. For example, Minnesota is "K." If you want to have Minnesota as your opponent, place "L" the second blank.

Note: Milwaukee, Minnesota, Philadelphia, and Houston must be played versus one of the following teams: Milwaukee, Philadelphia, Baltimore, San Francisco, Los Angeles, Chicago White Sox, or St. Louis.

Play in a Fantasy League!

Tommy Lasorda's worst nightmare may be this strange Fantasy League code in *Tommy Lasorda Baseball.* Just enter the code, choose your team, and get ready for some strange surprises (like the color of Tommy's face):

> VU9lrstpomXcZ
> TiebrHWyW

☆ Trampoline Terror ☆

Level Select and 99 Continues

Leap to greater heights with this *Trampoline Terror* code that'll enable you to choose any level and continue 99

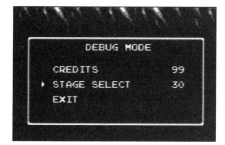

times. Wait until the Title screen appears and then simultaneously press Buttons A, B, C, Up, and then Start. You'll enter a selection screen where you can choose any level and select from 0–99 Continues.

⚔ Trouble Shooter ⚔

Stage Select

Skip through *Trouble Shooter* the easy way with this level select trick. Wait until the Title screen with the Start/Options selections appears. Next, simultaneously press Right, Button C, and Start on Controller 2. If you've performed the trick correctly, a stage select icon will appear on-screen. Now, simultaneously press Right, Button C, and Start to change the numbers until you reach the level number of your choice. Then, press Start to begin your mission.

✈ Truxton ✈

Boss Bustin'

Be a blow-hard with this trick that enables you to destroy the big bosses, or any enemy, in *Truxton* with just one bomb.

When you're ready to blast the enemy, push the bomb release button and then immediately pause your game. Stay paused for two or three seconds. Now, push the pause button two times, so the game un-pauses and then pauses again. Repeat this procedure until the bomb is gone. If this doesn't destroy your enemy, it only takes another shot or two to do him in.

✳ Turrican ✳

Bonus Options Menu

Here's a twisted trick that turns *Turrican* into a totally awesome treat. To access a special Options menu, go to the regular Options screen and select Exit. Now, press and hold Down on your control pad and press Button A, Button B two times, Button A, Button B, Button A two times, Button B, Button A two times, Button B, and Button A two times. The Option screen has special features, including a level select.

Power-Up at the Beginning of the Game

Snag a few quick Power-Ups at the beginning of *Turrican*. Instead of heading right at the beginning of the game, head left. A 1-Up will appear when you jump to the far left of the screen. When you move back to the right a box appears which spits out crystals every time you shoot it!

Special Bonus Items

After you beat the first boss in *Turrican* you'll probably need to power-up. When he's done for, move right until you reach some spikes. Unleash your Lightning Whip on the spikes to uncover some hidden blocks. Use the blocks to reach a bunch of 1-Ups, and then return and blow up the Power-Up blocks for extra fire power.

✪ Two Crude Dudes ✪

Twice the Continues

Need more Continues? Wait until your last life in *Two Crude Dudes* is just about to expire. Then, press Start on Controller 2. You're back on track with more Lives and Continues.

✂ Tyrants ✂

Passwords

Tyranize the world as Scarlet (leader of the people) with these *Tyrants* passwords:

> **2nd Epoch/148 Men:** NZUCWTIAEHV
> **3rd Epoch/184 Men:** ARTCKXKNMND
> **4th Epoch/176 Men:** YLGBUMQZKNL
> **5th Epoch/172 Men:** IHUBUGQULTB
> **6th Epoch/160 Men:** COCAKLDWEBX
> **7th Epoch/159 Men:** EBWROLJUHNJ
> **8th Epoch/163 Men:** QPIAXODAHHM
> **9th Epoch/143 Men:** ZBLDRNIHGTY
> **Mother of All Battles:** CPFDVMRBYST

⚐ Universal Soldier ⚐

Passwords

Here's a set of truly universal passwords that'll take this game's soldiers to any stage they like:

Stage 1-2: CHSGM	**Stage 3-1:** PKSND
Stage 1-3: MKSNS	**Stage 3-2:** CWBPM
Stage 2-1: SGGBY	**Stage 3-3:** SFTNP
Stage 2-2: JLGPH	**Stage 4-1:** CMVDG
Stage 2-3: JDRSD	**Stage 4-2:** BYTCM

Invincibility

The Universal Soldiers are tough, but they'll be even tougher when you give 'em an invincibility code. Enter the password: RWRZS.

☆ Valis ☆

Music Test

Check out the tunes in *Valis* with this code. Wait until the Title screen appears and then simultaneously press and hold Buttons A, B, and C, and press Start. A Music Selection screen will appear. Use any button to change the tune.

☀ Valis III ☀

Level Select

Here's a trick that enables you to choose any level you like in *Valis III*. Wait until the game's Title screen appears, and then simultaneously press Buttons A, B, C, Up, and Start. A map area will appear on-screen. Use Up and Down on your control pad to choose your level. Hit Start to begin the game.

Check Out the Animations

Here's a trick you can use to view any of *Valis III*'s animation sequences. Wait until the Title screen appears and then simultaneously press and hold Buttons A, C, Up, and Left, and then press Start. Now you can even watch the game's ending!

✈ Vapor Trail ✈

The Best Airplane

To have the best shot at beating *Vapor Trail*, make the Silph your flying vehicle of choice.

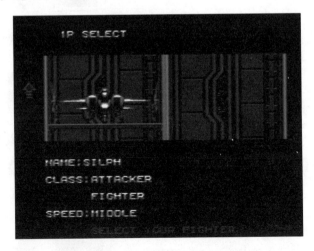

🏛 Warrior of Rome 🏛

Passwords

Use these passwords to battle on, brave *Warrior of Rome*:

Stage 2:	L3FHPOZNGW
Stage 3:	NXDS55JSWF
Stage 4:	O5TOJZSP5B

Ending Password

Victory is yours with this end password for *Warrior of Rome*:

GREBDWVNNE

♜ Warsong ♜

Scenario Select

At last, a trick that enables you to choose any level in *Warsong*. Begin a normal game, and then press Button A to reduce the map. Next, move the cursor to the upper left-hand corner of the screen. Now, move the cursor one space to the right and then one space down. Finally, press and hold Button B until a Scenario number appears. Use Up and Down on your control pad to pick a stage.

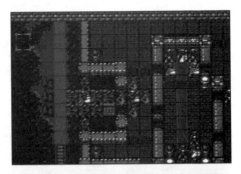

✸ X-Men ✸

Stage Select

Wait until you see this X-citing trick for the *X-men*. Plug a controller into only the first port. Next, press and hold Down, Button A, and Button C on your control pad while you turn on the system. Continue to hold all three buttons. When the "Press Start" screen appears, also press and hold Start. When the Difficulty Select screen appears, release all of the buttons. Choose any

difficulty and any character. When you enter the Danger Room, proceed to the right until you reach the area pictured in the screen. Each of the panels corresponds to a different stage in the game. When you're standing in front of your chosen level, simply press Down and then Button C on your control pad and you're off.

☻ Zombies Ate My Neighbors ☻

Passwords

Here are some ghoulish passwords for *Zombies Ate My Neighbors*:

Level 5: TYZR
Level 9: CBRK
Level 13: LCFJ
Level 17: BMLK
Level 21: VQBB
Level 25: QLNK
Level 29: QNKR
Level 33: SDHM
Level 37: BKVR
Level 41: BZPM
Level 45: VNYQ

★ Zoom! ★

Special Selection Screen

Zap to a special selection screen in *Zoom!*. When the One- or Two-Player screen appears, press Up, Up, Down, Down, Left, Right, Left, Right, Button A, and Button B. When you've completed the trick the special screen will appear.

Just for fun, select Debug from the Selection screen. When you begin to play the game hit Button A. The screen will split in two and reveal a screen full of numbers and letters—the game programming!

Part II

Yank the Cart Tricks!

Yank the Cart Tricks!

There's an entire category of strange Genesis tricks that involve yanking games out of your game system without turning the power off. Frequently, you'll have to try these tricks many times before you get them to work. While these tricks often work very well, you should keep the following in mind:

WARNING

**Yank the cart tricks can be very hazardous to your Genesis' health.
Any time you remove or insert games into your Genesis system with the power on, you risk permanently damaging your base unit. In other words, your Genesis could fry!! Perform these tricks at your own risk!**

♟ Alex Kidd in the Enchanted Castle ♟

Unlimited Lives

Don't kid around. Go for unlimited kidds in *Alex Kidd in the Enchanted Castle*. Insert *Space Harrier II* into your Genesis and go to the Options menu. Next, pull *Space Harrier II* out of your system without turning the power off. Finally, put *Alex Kidd in the Enchanted Castle* into your

Genesis (still without turning the power off) and you'll have unlimited lives! Note: This trick also works if you use *Super Thunder Blade*.

 Altered Beast

Unlimited Lives

Alter your game with unlimited Lives in *Altered Beast*. First, insert the game *Golden Axe* into your Genesis. Wait for the Sega Logo to appear on-screen, and then pull *Golden Axe* out of the Genesis

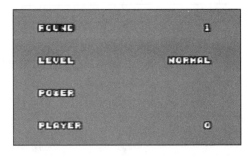

without turning the power off. Next, put *Altered Beast* into your system (still without turning the power off) and then hit Reset. To verify that the trick has worked, enter the Option mode and check to see if the player number is 0. If it is, you're armed with unlimited lives!

Endless Power

This trick gives you power that never stops in *Altered Beast*. Insert *Super Thunder Blade* into your Genesis. Wait until the Sega logo appears and then pull the game out without turning off your Genesis. Next, put *Altered Beast* into your Genesis (without turning the power off) and press Reset. When you begin play you'll notice that your stats are strange, but you'll have power that never decreases.

★ Batman ★

Unlimited Lives

Snag endless lives for the Caped Crusader in *Batman*. Insert any game into your Genesis. Wait until the Title screen appears and with the power on, pull the game out of your Genesis. Now, put *Batman* into your Genesis (without turning the power off), and press Reset.

⊕ E-SWAT ⊕

Level Select

E-SWAT is all you'll need to select any level in the game. Insert *E-SWAT* into your Genesis, turn on the power, and wait for the *E-SWAT* Title screen to appear. Next, remove *E-SWAT* from your system without turning off the power. Then, put *E-SWAT* back into your Genesis (without turning the power off) and press Reset. When the Information screen for Level 1 appears, press Start. Press and hold Left on your directional pad while simultaneously pressing Buttons A, B, and C. When a number appears on-screen, use Up or Down to choose your desired level.

★ Fantasia ✶

Unlimited Lives

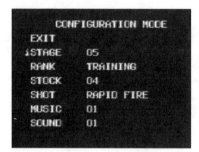

You'll need the game *Thunder Force II* to earn unlimited lives in *Fantasia*. Insert *Thunder Force II* into your Genesis, go to the Option screen (by pressing Button A and Start during the title screen) and select Level 5 of the training mission with five lives. Without turning the power off, pull *Thunder Force II* out of your Genesis. Next, put *Fantasia* back into your Genesis (still without turning the power off), and hit Reset. That's a little extra magic for Mickey.

☀ Ghouls 'n Ghosts ☀

Secret Title Screen

For a ghoulish surprise put *Super Thunder Blade* into your Genesis. Wait until the Sega logo appears and then pull *Super Thunder Blade* out of your system without turning the power off. Next, put *Ghouls 'n Ghosts* into your system (still without turning the power off) and press Reset. You'll see a Japanese Title screen!

♎ The Last Battle ♎

Level Select

Choose any level in *The Last Battle*. First, put a copy of *Space Harrier II* into your Genesis. When the Title screen appears, press Button A to reach a selection screen. Next, pull the game out of your Genesis without turning the power off. Insert *The Last Battle* (still without turning the power off), press Reset, and when the screen says "Legend of the Final Hero" simultaneously

press Buttons A, B, C, and Start. The words "Chapter 1" should appear on the screen. Use Up on your control pad to select different Chapters. When you've selected the Chapter of your choice, simply hit Start to begin the game.

♛ Mercs ♛

Level Select and Invincibility

Make your Merc invincible on the round of your choice with this yank the cart trick. Put *After Burner II* into your Genesis system and when the Sega sign appears remove it without turning the power off. Next, put *Mercs* into your system (still without turning the power off) and press Reset. Now you can choose any round in the Arcade or Original mode. To have complete control over the Merc, press and hold Buttons C and A and shoot with Button B. To become invincible, first select the round, then simultaneously press Buttons A, B, and C, and then press Start.

Erase the Original Best Players' Score

To wipe out the Best Players' Score in *Mercs*, simply put *Altered Beast* into your Genesis system. When the Sega sign appears, pull the game out of your Genesis without turning the power off. Next, insert *Mercs* (still without turning off the power) and press Reset. Now go and rewrite history!

⊕ Moonwalker ⊕

Invincibility

Nobody can touch a hair on Michael's head with this invincibility trick for *Moonwalker*. Put *Space Harrier II* into your

Genesis and then, when the Title screen appears, remove it without turning off the power. Now, still without turning the power off, put *Moonwalker* into your Genesis. Press Reset, begin play, and you're invincible.

∩ Phelios ∩

Expert Mode

You'll need *Golden Axe* to play a special Expert mode in *Phelios*. Put *Golden Axe* into your Genesis and when the Title screen appears remove it without turning off the

power. Now insert *Phelios* (still without turning the power off) and press Reset. Voilà, Expert Mode!

𝕏 Rambo III 𝕏

Unlimited Lives

Make Rambo more macho than ever with this unlimited lives trick. Put *Altered Beast* into your Genesis. Wait for the Title screen with the statues to appear and then remove *Altered Beast* from your Genesis without turning the power off. Next, put *Rambo III* into your Genesis (still without turning the power off) and then press Reset and Start. You've got unlimited Lives.

☆ Revenge of Shinobi ☆

Turn Revenge of Shinobi into Super Shinobi

To transform *Revenge of Shinobi* into Super Shinobi put any other game into your Genesis system, and then remove it without turning the power off. Next, put *Revenge of Shinobi* into your Genesis (still without turning the power off) and press Reset. You'll see the Super Shinobi Title screen!!

★ Space Harrier II ★

Begin with 99 Lives

If you're feeling harried, use this trick to begin *Space Harrier II* with 99 Lives. First, put *Altered Beast* into your Genesis. When the screen appears with pictures of all the statues, pull the game out of your Genesis without turning off the power. The screen freezes. Next, without turning the power off, put *Space Harrier II* into your Genesis. The screen should stay frozen, but you'll hear strange out-of-tempo music. Hit Reset and the Sega logo appears, followed by the *Space Harrier II* title screen. Begin play as you normally would. Instead of four lives you'll have 99!

★ Spider-Man ★

Super Spider-Man

Your spidey senses will tingle when you see that this trick's gonna give you 60 web cartridges, invincibility, and the ability to skip levels! Put *Strider* into your Genesis. When the purple word appears in the background, pull the game

out of your Genesis without turning off the power. Next, put *Spider-Man* into your Genesis (still without turning the power off) and press Reset. Select the Option mode. If you see "(!!!)" on-screen you've done the trick correctly. When your game begins you've already got 60 web cartridges. To activate Invincibility press Start to pause your game and then simultaneously press Buttons B and C and then resume your game. Your Invincibility lasts for about six seconds. If you *do* run low on web fluid, press Start to pause your game, press Button A, and then return to your game. Finally, if you want to skip levels press Start to pause your game and then simultaneously press Buttons A, B, and C. Each time you press this combo you'll skip a level in the game.

☭ Strider ☭

Unlimited Lives

Why not stroll through *Strider* with unlimited Lives? Insert *Altered Beast* into your Genesis and when the Title screen appears, remove it without turning off the power. Next, put *Strider* into your Genesis (still without turning the power off) and

press Reset. When you begin your game the Player Remaining counter will read nine and will stay at nine!

✳ Streets of Rage ✳

Tons of Lives

Fight on with 15 or more Lives with each Continue in *Streets of Rage*. Put Streets of Rage into your Genesis and when the Sega logo appears, remove the game without turning the power off. Next, put *Streets of Rage* back into your Genesis (still without turning the power off) and press Reset. Go to the Options screen and the game's difficulty should read "6677." Choose your controller button functions and exit the Option mode to begin your game. You'll begin with nine Lives, and the Lives counter shouldn't begin to count down until you've died several times.

Note: Some of the game's text may also convert to Japanese.

✦ Thunder Force II ✦

Stage Select

To select from Stages 1–9 in *Thunder Force II* you'll need the cartridge *Target Earth*.

Insert *Target Earth* into your Genesis, enter the Options menu, and change "Pad Reset" to "Enable." Return to the main screen and wait for the demo to appear.

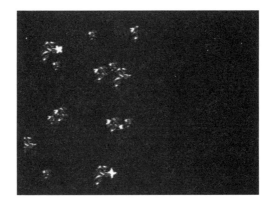

When the green enemies begin to fire during the demo, pull *Target Earth* out of your Genesis without turning the power off. Now, put *Thunder Force II* into your Genesis (still without turning the power off).

Press Reset and the letters "MD" should appear alongside of the Title screen. Simultaneously Press Button A and Start to go to the Options screen. Use Left and Right on your control pad to choose any stage from 1 to 9.

CONFIGURATION MODE
EXIT
iSTAGE   09
RANK
STOCK   97
SHOT   NORMAL SHOT
MUSIC   99
SOUND   41

Part III

Action Replay and Pro Action Replay

Hardware-Helpers*

If you can't make it past that level, bust that boss, or figure out how to survive that barrage of enemy fire, you just might want to read this section. There's an entire line of game-busting products, hardware-helpers as it were, that'll give you an unbeatable edge. Our favorites are the Action Replay and Pro Action Replay. Check them out!

Made by Datel Electronics, the Action Replay and Action Replay: Pro Version work with Genesis or Mega Drive games (they come with Mega Drive adaptors) and make magic happen with your favorite video games.

The Action Replay is a snap to install. Simply connect your cart to the device, then plug the Replay into your Genesis. Now the fireworks begin. A code book, which comes bundled with the Replay, contains "cheat" listings for approximately 50 games. Typical codes include Extra Lives, Invincibility, Level Warps, and instant Power-Ups. You can key in up to four codes at the Parameter screen, and use the Enable switch to activate and deactivate the codes' effects.

Unfortunately, some of the codes apply to Japanese carts only. Although the initial code selection was limited, we've got an expanded list for you on the following pages.

The regular Action Replay is shock therapy for your Genesis, but there's a hard-core model that could fry its microchips! The Action Replay: Pro Version has an awesome feature—user-friendly programmability.

In this version, the Enable switch has a third setting called "Trainer." Flick it on and you can use five different techniques to find your game's codes—Countable Number, Timer, Energy, Status, and Slow but Sure. Each is different in execution, but the principle is the same. You play your game, isolate a statistic, and feed that statistic's numerical value into the Action Replay. You keep changing the numerical value until the Trainer isolates a beneficial code.

For example, if you want Extra Lives in Strider, you enter your starting lives (five) into the Trainer. The Trainer looks for the number five in Strider's program. Then you play the game, lose a life, and provide the number four. Repeat this process until the Trainer discovers Strider's life code.

The Pro Version won't pull off really weird code creations, such as a skywalking Sonic, but the techniques help resourceful users create basic cheats for nearly any game. The Trainer is a great complement to the codes documented in the manual.

*Reprinted with permission from *GamePro* Magazine, June, 1992

Action Replay Codes

✦ After Burner II ✦

Burn up the skies with these codes:

> **Infinite Lives:**
> 002D5 06004
> **Infinite Missiles:**
> 00381 C600A

💥 Altered Beast 💥

Here's a beastly code:

> **Almost Invulnerable:**
> 002C5 8603E

☆ Arrow Flash ☆

Stick these codes into your bow and go for it:

> **Ten Special Weapons per Life:** 00A5C E000A
> **Unlimited Special Weapons:** 00BA3 06004
> **Unlimited Lives:** 00554 46004

★ Batman ★

Here's a few extra boosts for the Caped Crusader:

> **Infinite Lives:** 004B5 46002
> **Invincibility:** 01016 26008
> **Extra Bullets and Rockets:** 0018F 400FF
> **Infinite Rockets and Bullets:** 0068E 66002
> **Infinite Rockets for Bat Car:** 00696 A6002
> **Infinite Rockets for Bat Plane:** 0069A E6002
> **Skip Levels:** 000BB 64E71 (Disable the Action
>   Replay when you reach your level of choice)

✐ Bonanza Brothers ✐

Eureka! It's a bonanza of codes:

> **Infinite Lives for the Red**
>   **Player:** 00539 E6068
> **Infinite Lives for the Blue**
>   **Player:** 00542 A606C
> **Five Minutes Per Level:**
>   0104B E0005
> **Infinite Time:** 0106D 04A28

⊕ Buck Rogers ⊕

Here's a healthy pick-me-up for Buck:

> **First Generated**
> **Character Keeps a**
> **Constant Health**
> **of 99:** FFC47 E0063

Castle of Illusion
★ Starring Mickey Mouse ★

Make Mickey a star with this code:

> **Mickey Only Takes One Damage Point per Section:**
> 00B79 44E75 (He still falls off cliffs.)

⚔ Crackdown ⚔

Andy and Ben really Crackdown with these codes:

> **Gives Ben Unlimited Machine Gun Bullets:**
>   02821 06002
> **Gives Andy Unlimited Machine Gun Bullets:**
>   0282C A6002
> **Gives Ben Unlimited Cannon Shots:** 0281F 26002
> **Gives Andy Unlimited Cannon Shots:** 0282A C6002
> **Gives Ben Unlimited Super Bombs:** 00584 E6004
> **Gives Andy Unlimited Super Bombs:** 0057B C6004
> **Combined Gives Ben Infinite Lives:** 00D6E 46004
>   and 00208 66004

Combined Gives Andy Infinite Lives: 00D82 C6004
and 00212 E6004
Infinite Time: 000D0 A6004

⬦ DecapAttack ⬦

These codes will give Chuck the help he needs to *DecapAttack*:

Chuck Is Immune to Enemy Attack: 02EC9 E6002
Allows Chuck to Walk on Lava: 02B16 66002
Removes All Enemies from the Game: 02EC3 86004
Infinite Chucks: 02EB8 84E71
Use to Skip through Levels: 02EB6 26002

(Enter this code and then when the game begins, activate the Action Replay. Your game will start to skip levels. When you reach the right level, disable the Action Replay.)

⬓ Desert Strike ⬓

Here's codes that'll give you the power you need to storm *Desert Strike*:

Infinite Lives:
006AA 44A79
Unlimited Fuel:
00689 C4A79
Bonus Armor:
0049D 07FFF

★ El Viento ★

Power-up with these codes:

> **Stops Player from Taking Damage**
> **from Most Enemies:** 00C47 64A79
> **Keeps Flame Weapon at Full**
> **Strength All the Time:** 00940 24A79

★ Fantasia ★

Use these codes to make *Fantasia* more than just a Mickey Mouse game:

> **Most Enemies Will Give You Energy:**
> 005D5 4103C and 005D5 84E71
> **Infinite Large Magic:** 00622 84E71
> **Infinite Little Magic:** 00625 04E71

★ Fatal Rewind★

Don't make the deadly mistake of not trying these codes:

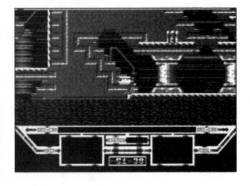

Infinite Lives:
  02B6D 66002 and
  02E39 A6002
Invulnerable: 02898
  04E71

(If you get stuck in the goo, you may have to turn the Replay off or a moment)

✹ Ghostbusters ✹

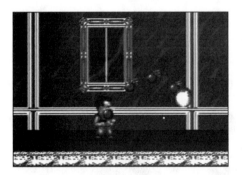

You'll have more than just a ghost of a chance with these codes:

Gives You Lots of Money for Use in Shops:
  014D3 06008
Gives Your Player an Unlimited Amount of
  Bombs: 006D4 26004
Gives Your Player Infinite Lives: 0088E 26004

✦ Hellfire ✦

Burn up the screen
with these codes:

> **Infinite Lives:** 00284 86004
>
> **Unlimited Super Weapons:** 002AE E6004
>
> **Power-up Completely When You Collect Your
> First "P":** 00262 C33FC and 00262 E0005

☀ The Immortal ☀

Immortalize yourself with these codes:

> **Infinite Lives:** 0081E 8197C and 0081E A00FF
>
> **Defeat Goblins in Combat:** 0113F 46006
>
> **Beat Floor Traps, Worms, Arrows, etc:** 00993 04E75

⊷ James Pond ⊶

Things will go swim-
mingly with these
codes:

> **Infinite Lives:**
> 007ED A6004
> **Infinite Time:**
> 008A1 66002

James Pond II:
⊷ Codename Robocod ⊶

Kick some tale fin with these codes:

> **Infinite Lives:** 00190 A4E71
>
> **Protection Against Enemies:** 003D1 C6002
>
> **Protection Against Spikes:** 003CC 26002
>
> (All of these codes combined make you invincible!)

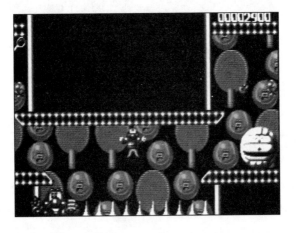

◈ Kid Chameleon ◈

Give the Kid a break with these codes:

> **Stop the Timer:**
> 00BEA 84A78
>
> **Infinite Lives:**
> 00B83 84A78
>
> **Immunity to Enemies:**
> 00B73 44A78
>
> **Diamonds = 7 points:**
> 00FE3 65E78

★ The Last Battle ★

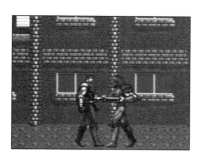

It won't be your *Last Battle* when you use these cool codes:

> **Infinite Energy:**
> 0093D 86002
>
> **Infinite Time:**
> 00121 C6002

♟ Mercs ♟

Make your *Mercs* mighty with these codes:

> **Infinite Bombs:** 0080B 8C351
> **Infinite Energy:** 00B09 44E71

☆ Moonwalker ☆

These codes enable Michael to easily "Beat It" to the end of the game:

> **Gives Michael Increased Dance Ability:**
> 005F1 E31FC and 005F2 00040

(If your energy gets low while you're using this code, just press your special power button—usually Button A—and Michael will have full power again.)

• Ms. Pac-Man •

Don't pack it in, use this code instead:

> **Infinite Pac-Women:**
> 00183 66002

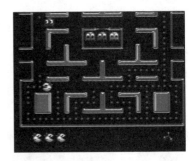

☆ Mystic Defender ☆

Here are a few mystical codes to help you defeat the game:

> **Makes Firing Super-Charged Weapons Easier:**
> 00C0D E4E71 (All you have to do is press the fire button and release.)
> **Protects You Against Most Enemy Attacks:**
> 006EF 06002

✭ QuackShot Starring Donald Duck ✭

You'll quack up when you see all these great codes:

Start with Seven Lives: 00502 60007

Start with Nine Lives: 00502 60009

(Note: By changing the last couple of digits in this code, you can change the number of Lives you wish to start with.)

Infinite Lives: 00481 E6004

Invulnerable to Enemy Attack: 005E1 0600C

Donald Doesn't Calm Down Until the End of a Level When He Loses His Temper or Until You Turn Off the Action Replay: 005FD E6002

Donald Loses His Temper After Only One Chili Pepper: 007D0 E0001

Begin the Game with About 15 Units of Popcorn: 00503 C31C2

Once You Grab Popcorn, It Never Decreases: 00510 86002

★ Raiden Trad ★

Blaze through the skies with these codes:

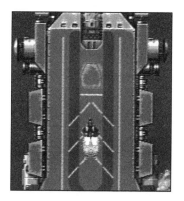

Begin Each Life with 10 Bombs: 003EB 6000A

Begin Your Game with 20 Lives: 000A5 A7014

Begin Your Game with 127 Lives: 000A5 A707F

⚔ Rambo III ⚔

With this code Rambo's got what it takes to beat the game:

> **Large Number of Lives:** 00228 03CC0

✲ Revenge of Shinobi ✲

Get your revenge with these great Shinobi codes:

> **Gives You 99 Lives in the Easy Setting of the Game:** 0090F 40063 (You must go to the Options screen for the new value to be accepted.)
>
> **Infinite Lives:** 009E4 66002
>
> **Invulnerable in One Direction:** 00B4E 86000
>
> **Invulnerable in the Other Direction:** 00B57 E6000 (Combined, these two codes give immunity to enemy attack, but not to falling off the screen.)
>
> **Unlimited Normal Shurikens:** 00B93 E6002
>
> **Unlimited Super Shurikens:** 00C0E 24E71

✰ Road Rash ✰

Take to the streets with this code:

> **Slows Game Down When Action Replay Is On:** 00BA7 C6002

★ Shadow Dancer ★

You won't have a shadow of a doubt with these codes:

> **Large Amount of Lives:** 01029 E7200
> **Unlimited Magic:** 00ADD 213C1

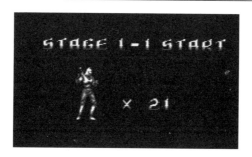

⊛ Sonic the Hedgehog ⊛

There'll be a sonic boom when you fire up these codes:

> **Makes Sonic Invulnerable to Enemies, Bullets, and Spikes Until He Picks Up Another Shield:** 0039F 011C1
>
> **Aerial View of a Level:** 0039F C31C1
> (You can also place objects by pressing Button A and placing them with Button C. When you're finished press Button B and you'll continue.)

Gives Sonic Turbo Shoes with Every TV He Breaks: 00A35 E6042

Begin with Several Hundred Rings on Each Level: 0039D C31C1

Begin in Any Level: 00324 26010
(When you press Start you'll be prompted by a Level Select screen that enables you to choose any level.)

Begin the Game with 99 Lives: 00334 A0063

Infinite Lives: 0138A 06032

• Speedball 2 •

You'll flash right through the game with this well-rounded code:

Unlimited Money:
0061F A6004 and
00654 26004

⊕ Spider-Man ⊕

Spidey's in good shape with these cool codes:

Each Shot Increases Your Webs Slightly:
016A9 E526D

Gives a Bit of Web Energy Each Time You Use the Shield: 016C9 2506D

Improved Shield: 016CA 80300

Your Shield Is Activated Whenever It's Needed: 0183C 86006

✴ Streets of Rage ✸

Use these codes to heat up the *Streets of Rage*:

Infinite Lives for Both Players: 002B6 64E71
Infinite Time on Each Section: 010CE 01C80
Constant Supply of Special Weapons: 00402 E4E71

☭ Strider ☭

Save Strider's skin with these codes:

Infinite Lives: 020A1 C6002
Infinite Time to Complete a Level: 002BC E4E71
Large Amounts of Energy for Each Man: 0011F 8007F
(You should avoid picking up extra energy icons as you may find that they'll bring you back to normal energy.)

Sword of Sodan

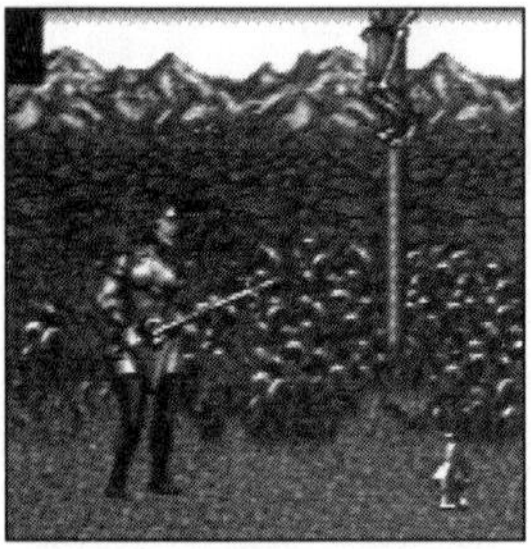

Sword play is a little easier with this code:

Infinite Lives: 00474 26002
(Remember to use the flaming brand towards the end of the game. If you use it too early you'll be stuck!)

Task Force Harrier

Clear the skies with these flighty codes:

Infinite Lives: 0024F 64A38
Infinite Bombs: 0021B 24A38
Always Keep Extra Aircraft: FF810 60001
Activate Action Replay for Extra Aircraft: 00204 86002

Thunder Force II

Force your enemies off the screen with these codes:

Begin with 255 Lives: 0009D 431FC and 0009D 600FF
Do Not Lose Selected Weapons When Destroyed: 0041C E6002

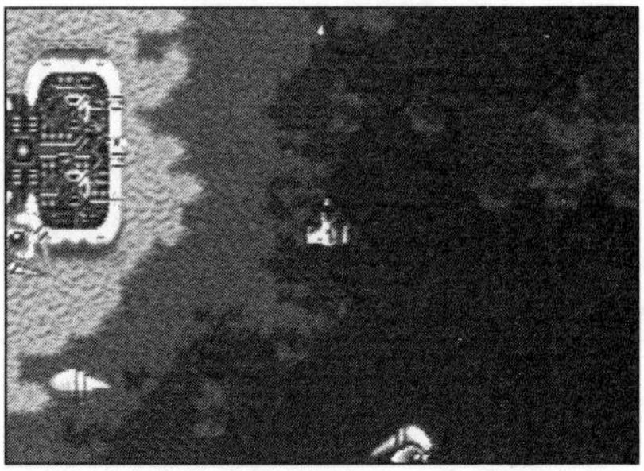

★ ToeJam & Earl ✫

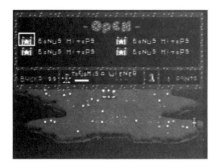

Give the two dudes from outer space a lift with these funky codes:

> **Infinite Lives in Most Circumstances:**
> 00BCB 06002
> **Begins ToeJam with a Total of 99 Bucks:**
> 00BB9 80063
> **Begins Earl with a Total of 99 Bucks:**
> 00BBB C0063

♣ Truxton

Soar with these super codes:

> **Begin with Over 400 Ships:** 000A8 61040
> **Begin with Over 4,000 Bombs:** 000AB 41040

PRO ACTION REPLAY Codes

♟ Alex Kidd in the Enchanted Castle ♟

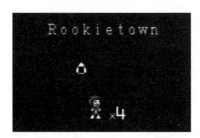

The Kidd saves the day with the Enchanted Castle code:

> **Infinite Lives:** FFC12 00005

⚖ Alien Storm ⚖

Weather the storm with these codes:

> **Turn on Action Replay Each Time You Need to Restore Your Life:** FFCE0 B0060
>
> **Unlimited Energy:** FFCE0 C0080
>
> **Full Energy and Life Bar:** 00352 A31FC and 00352 CFFFF
>
> **Unlimited Continues:** 003A2 E6002

≋ Bimini Run ≋

Cruise through the waters of *Bimini Run* with this code:

FF3BA 50006

★ Burning Force ★

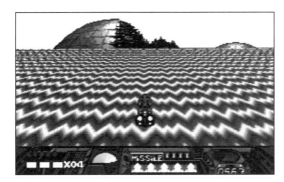

Set yourself on fire with this cool code:

Gives You 40 Lives on Reset:
FFB25 C0004

⚔ Captain America and the Avengers ⚔

Avenge Captain America the easy way:

Unlimited energy:
· FF9F0 B0064

Castle of Illusion
★ Starring Mickey Mouse ☆

Mickey won't have any illusions with this code:

> **Infinite Lives:** FFF32 50003

𝕏 Chuck Rock 𝕏

Chuck really rocks with these codes:

> **Unlimited Lives:** FF06D 10003

• Crue Ball •

You'll have a ball when you plug in this one:

> **Unlimited Ball:**
> FF843 D0003

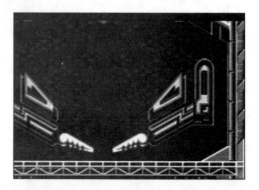

♜ Dark Castle ♜

Come into the light with this code:

> **Infinite Lives:** FF130 B0003

◈ Death Duel ◈

Duel to the death with ease thanks to this passcode:

> **Unlimited Tries:**
> FFFF2 90005

★ Dick Tracy ★

Calling all cars, Dick Tracy's not gonna' need your help now that he's got these codes:

> **Begin with 99 Lives:** FFFD6 10064
> **Infinite Time:** FFFD7 10059

● DinoLand ●

Here's a prehistoric code:

> **Infinite Balls:**
> FFF5A 30003

★ DJ Boy ★

Use this code to skate straight to victory:

> **Infinite Lives:**
> FFA18 90004

🚁 Earnest Evans 🚁

Evans is earnest about winning with this one:

> **Unlimited Men:**
> FFA4A F0002

🐟 Ecco the Dolphin 🐟

Ecco's a porpoise with a pupose when you plug in these codes:

> **Health Meter Stays the Same:** FFB63 50038
> **Air Meter Stays the Same:** FFB63 60003

⚛ Ex-Mutants ⚛

Your mutants will have an ex-cellent chance for victory when you use this code:

> **Unlimited Men:**
> FF006 B0003

💥 Fatal Rewind 💥

Don't get too wound up. Use these codes instead:

GET READY
TO DIE

> **First Laser Picked Up Is Kept Until the End of the Level:** FF5B3 D0007
>
> **First Triple Picked Up Is Kept Until the End of the Level:** FF5B4 90007
>
> **First Side Shot Picked Up Is Kept Until the End of the Level:** FF4B3 F0008
>
> **First Mine Sweeper Picked Up Is Kept Until the End of the Level:** FF4B4 D0008
>
> **Infinite Lives:** 02B6D 66002 and 02E39 A6002
>
> **Invincibility:** 02898 04E71

✦ Fire Shark ✦

Fly right with these codes:

> **Infinite Lives:** FF028 70003
> **Infinite Bombs:** FF042 B0003

★ Gaiares ★

Go on a space shooting spree:

> **Unlimited Men:** FFF3E 10004

✕ Galahad ✕

You'll be knighted when you use these Galahad codes:

> **Unlimited Men:**
> FF13F 70005

☆ Ghouls 'n Ghosts ☆

Here's a spooky code:

> **Infinite Time:** FFB04 90030

✦ Global Gladiators ✦

Clean up the environment and the game with this trio of codes:

> **Unlimited Time:** FF001 C0035
> **Unlimited Energy:** FFFED 2000A
> **Unlimited Men:** FF00B 40033

✕ Golden Axe ✕

Get into the swing of things with this code:

> **Infinite Lives:**
> FFFE7 C0003

✗ Golden Axe II ✗

Take a hack at the game
with these helpful codes:

Infinite Lives:
FF088 00002

**Always Keep Five
Bombs:**
FF088 20005

⚔ Granada ⚔

Score big with this code:

Invincible: FFB45 70009

● Green Dog ●

Ya mon! Try this code:

Unlimited Men:
FF17D D0004
Unlimited Energy:
FF258 D0030

⊟ Hard Drivin' ⊟

Cruise straight through the game with this cool code:

> **Unlimited Time:**
> FF567 E0059

★ Immortal ★

Immortal won't seem quite so creepy with these codes:

> **Unlimited Continues on Most Levels:** FF109 A0002
> **Unlimited Fireballs When Selected:** FF0B7 20003
> **No Energy Loss During Fights:** FF10A 8000C

✸ Insector X ✸

Here's a code that takes the sting out of the game:

> **Infinite Lives:**
> FF980 30007

● Junction ●

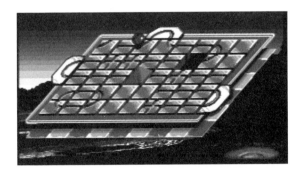

Connect in a big way with this *Junction* code:

> **25 Balls or Infinite Balls on Reset:** FFCCA 70019

⊕ Kid Chameleon ⊕

No need to Kid around with these codes:

Level Select Code: FFFC4 500XX

(Input the level number in XX. For example, to play Level 6, enter 50006)

Maximum Number of Diamonds: FFFC4 30063

Infinite Lives: FFFC3 F0080

◉ Klax ◉

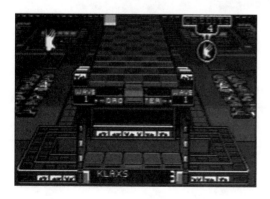

Things will click in *Klax* with this code:

Infinite Lives:
FF0FD D0014

♦ Krusty's Fun House ♦

Now Krusty can really have some fun:

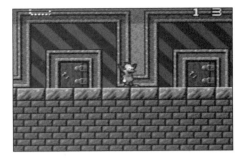

> **Unlimited Men:**
> FFOFF 30003

⚖ The Last Battle ⚖

Use these codes to make it your *Last Battle*:

> **Time Set with Last Two Numbers:**
> FFFE1 50099
> **Infinite Lives:**
> FFFE0 D0048

★ Lightening Force ★

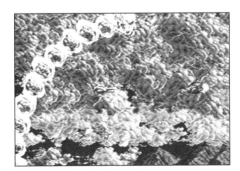

Zap the enemy with this forceful code:

> **Unlimited Men:**
> FFF2F 10003

★ Little Mermaid ★

Beach Ursula with this Mermaid code:

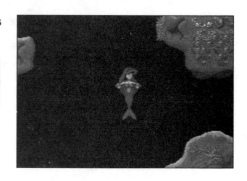

> **Unlimited Energy:**
> FFA61 10028

● Marble Madness ●

You'll roll straight through the game with this code:

> **Infinite Time:** FFB0C F0038

✦ M.U.S.H.A. ✦

M.U.S.H.A. won't be a shot in the dark with this code:

> **Infinite Lives:**
> FFD11 30003

🯁 OutRun 🯁

Pick up the pace with this *OutRun* code:

> **Time Set with Last Two Numbers:**
> FFFE1 50099

⚖ Paperboy ⚖

This code really delivers:

> **Unlimited Men:**
> FFC04 F0005

∩ Phelios ∩

Use these devilish codes to defeat *Phelios*:

> **Infinite Lives:**
> FFF47 30003
> **Invincibility:**
> FFF47 50003

Pit-Fighter

Get ready to pit yourself against the best with this scrappy code:

Infinite Energy:
FF2B7 F00D8

Predator 2

Hunt down the Predator with this code:

Unlimited Men:
FF027 C0002

Road Blasters

Shift into gear with this code:

Infinite Lives:
FF2A5 D0005

★ Rolling Thunder 2 ★

Take a shot at *Rolling Thunder 2* with these codes:

Infinite Lives: FFF20 D0002
Infinite Bullets: FFF20 30040
Infinite Machine Gun: FFF20 50029
Infinite Time: FFF13 50074
Invincibility: FFCD3 30001

✸ Shadow of the Beast ✸

Here's a beastly code that'll up your energy:

Unlimited Energy:
FF1A1 7000C

✳ Side Pocket ✳

Take a cue from this cool code:

> **Cool Shot:**
> FFC09 40008

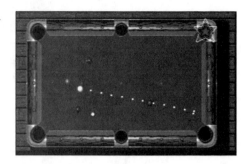

⊕ Slaughter Sport ⊕

Slaughter is sport with this sly code:

> **Unlimited Energy:**
> FF2C3 00003

✦ Sol-Deace ✦

Shoot straight with this *Sol-Deace* code:

> **Unlimited Men:**
> FFA0A 50004

❊ Sonic the Hedgehog 2 ❊

Hog the screen with these Sonic codes:

> **Always have 224 Rings:** FFFE2 100E0
> **Unlimited Time:** FFFE2 40007

⬆ Space Harrier II ⬆

Don't space out. Use this code instead:

> **Unlimited Men:** FFF20 50005

⊕ Spider-Man ⊕

Spin a web of deceit with this code:

> **Unlimited Time:** FFE69 1003B

✸ Splatterhouse 2 ✸

You'll splatter the creeps with this code combo:

Unlimited Energy:
FF00F 70003
Unlimited Lives:
FF00F 80003

🏛 Stormlord 🏛

Expect clear skies with this code:

Infinite Lives:
FF025 50005

🎛 Super Hang-On 🎛

Hang on to your pride with this timely code:

Set Your Time with the Last Two Numbers of This Code: FF055 40099

Super Thunder Blade

Chop up the skies with this life-saving code:

Infinite Lives:
FFF82 A0007

Sword of Sodan

Sword play the easy way:

Unlimited Lives:
FF13A F0005

T2: The Arcade Game

You'll be back again and again with this code:

Unlimited Continues:
FF80C A0004

⬧ Tailspin ⬧

Kick some tail with this code:

> **Unlimited Men:** FF27C D0002

⚚ The Terminator ⚚

Hasta la vista, baby:

> **Unlimited Energy:**
> FF147 D001F

⬧ Toki ⬧

Swing from the trees with this code:

> **Unlimited Men:**
> FF1B8 60005
> **Unlimited Time:**
> FF1B6 30059

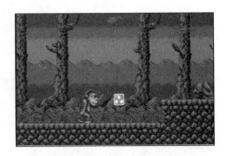

✷ Trampoline Terror ✷

Jump out of trouble with this bouncy code:

> **Infinite Lives:** FFF70 90004

✎ Trouble Shooter ✎

Eliminate all problems with these trouble-free codes:

> **Infinite Lives:** FFFE2 10005
> **Infinite Magic:** FFB7F 90008

🚁 Twin Cobra 🚁

You'll have double the fun with this pair of codes:

> **Infinite Lives:** FFB29 F0005
> **Infinite Bombs:** FFB28 60003

◗ Two Crude Dudes ◗

The dudes won't have to be crude with this code:

> **Unlimited Energy:**
> FF475 70032

¥ Universal Soldier ¥

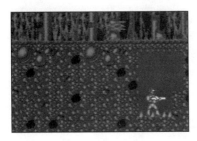

You'll have all the Universal Soldiers you need with this code:

> **Unlimited Men:**
> FF0AD F0003

⊕ Wardner ⊕

Ward off any problems with this life-giving code:

> **Infinite Lives:** FF829 40004

✦ Whip Rush ✦

Take a crack at the game with this snappy code:

> **Infinite Lives:**
> FFD02 80005

✰ Wings of Wor ✰

Soar through the game with this high-flying code:

> **Invincibility:** FFD6C D0004

World of Illusion
⊕ Starring Mickey Mouse ⊕

It's not a Mickey Mouse
game any more:

> **Unlimited Energy:**
> FFA03 80005
> **Unlimited Continues:**
> FFFD5 30003

⚑ Zany Golf ⚑

Tee off in a big way
with this zany code:

> **15 Balls or Infinite
> Balls on Reset:**
> FFE9A 2000F

★ Zoom! ★

Zip through *Zoom* with
this code:

> **Infinite Lives:**
> FFF00 B0003

SECRETS OF THE GAMES BOOKS

VIDEO GAME BOOKS

Nintendo Games Secrets, Volumes 1, 2, 3, and 4	$12.95 each
Nintendo Game Boy Secrets, Volumes 1 and 2	$12.95 each
Sega Genesis Secrets, Volumes 1, 2, 3, 4, and 5	$12.95 each
Official Sega Genesis Power Tips Book, 2nd Edition (in full color!)	$14.95
TurboGrafx-16 and TurboExpress Secrets, Volumes 1 and 2	$11.95 each
Super NES Games Secrets, Volumes 1, 2, 3, and 4	$12.95 each
GamePro Presents:	
Nintendo Games Secrets Greatest Tips	$11.95
Sega Genesis Games Secrets Greatest Tips	$11.95
Super NES Games Secrets Greatest Tips	$11.95
Super Mario World Game Secrets	$12.95
The Legend of Zelda:	
A Link to the Past Game Secrets	$12.95
Super Star Wars Official Game Secrets	$12.95
Super Empire Strikes Back Official Games Secrets	$12.95
Secrets of Mana Official Games Secrets	$12.95

And there's a lot more
where these came from...

COMPUTER GAME BOOKS

SimEarth: The Official Strategy Guide	$19.95
Harpoon Battlebook: The Official Strategy Guide	$19.95
Wing Commander I and II:	
The Ultimate Strategy Guide	$19.95
Chuck Yeager's Air Combat Handbook	$19.95
The Official Lucasfilm Games	
Air Combat Strategies Book	$19.95
Sid Meier's Civilization,	
or Rome on 640K a Day	$19.95
Ultima: The Avatar Adventures	$19.95
Ultima VII and Underworld: More Avatar Adventures	$19.95
JetFighter II: The Official Strategy Guide	$19.95
A-Train: The Official Strategy Guide	$19.95
PowerMonger: The Official Strategy Guide	$19.95
Global Conquest: The Official Strategy Guide (w/disk)	$24.95
Falcon 3: The Official Combat Strategy Book (w/disk)	$27.95
Dynamix Great War Planes:	
The Ultimate Strategy Guide	$19.95
Gunship 2000: The Authorized Strategy Guide	$19.95
SimLife: The Official Strategy Guide	$19.95
Stunt Island: The Official Strategy Guide	$19.95
Populous: The Official Strategy Guide	$19.95
Prince of Persia: The Official Strategy Guide	$19.95
X-wing: The Official Strategy Guide	$19.95
Empire Deluxe: The Official Strategy Guide	$19.95
F-15 Strike Eagle III: The Official Strategy Guide	$24.95
The 7th Guest: The Official Strategy Guide	$19.95

TO ORDER BOOKS ONLY

Please send me the following items:

Quantity	Title	Unit Price	Total
_____	_____	$_____	$_____
_____	_____	$_____	$_____
_____	_____	$_____	$_____
_____	_____	$_____	$_____
_____	_____	$_____	$_____
_____	_____	$_____	$_____
_____	_____	$_____	$_____

Subtotal $_____

7.25% SALES TAX California only $_____

SHIPPING and HANDLING* $_____

TOTAL ORDER $_____

*$4.00 shipping and handling charge for the first book, and 50¢ for each additional book.

HOW TO ORDER

By telephone:
With Visa or MC, call **(916) 632-4400** . Mon.–Fri. 9–4 PST.
By Mail: Just fill out the information below and send with your remittance.

My name is_____

I live at_____

City_____ State_____ ZIP_____

Visa/MC#_____Exp._____

Signature_____

PRIMA PUBLISHING
P.O. Box 1260BK
Rocklin, CA 95677
(satisfaction unconditionally guaranteed)